FANTASY IN FLORENCE

Leaving Home and Loving it

ROD McQUEEN

ILLUSTRATED BY SANDY McQUEEN

McArthur & Company
Toronto

First published in Canada in 2007 by
McArthur & Company
322 King St. West, Suite 402
Toronto, ON   M5V 1J2
www.mcarthur-co.com

Library and Archives Canada Cataloguing in Publication

McQueen, Rod, 1944- _   Fantasy in Florence / Rod McQueen.

ISBN 978-1-55278-643-7

1. McQueen, Rod, 1944- --Travel--Italy--Florence.
2. Florence _(Italy)--Description and travel. I. Title.
DG734.23.M35 2007   914.5'510493   C2007-900868-2

Cover and interior: *Mad Dog Design*

Printed in Canada by *Friesens*

The publisher would like to acknowledge the financial support of the
Government of Canada through the Book Publishing Industry
Development Program (BPIDP) and the Canada Council for our publishing
activities. The publisher further wishes to acknowledge the financial
support of the Ontario Arts Council for our publishing program.

10 9 8 7 6 5 4 3 2 1

FANTASY IN FLORENCE

To all our friends in Florence:
Grazie mille

INTRODUCTION

"*BUON GIORNO*, SIGNOR MCQUEEN," calls the man, threading his way through the crowded sidewalk. Sandy and I are easy to spot, all crumpled and luggage-laden, after the airport taxi leaves us squinting in the bright September sunlight of central Florence. Roberto Bianchi introduces himself and then leads us past Luisa Via Roma, an upscale fashion boutique, into a gray stone building with a central atrium containing an ancient wood-and-glass elevator that creaks as it carries us up. Our new landlord, a gracious gray-haired man in his early sixties, speaks no English. Despite some language lessons, I have too little Italian, but my French is about equal to his, so that's how we converse.

On the fourth floor, we wait impatiently while Signor Bianchi produces a clatter of keys for the two locks and opens the apartment door. "*Prego*," he says, indicating we should precede him. We head directly for the living-room window, where we gaze in amazement at the panoramic view that we had seen on the Internet. Less than two hundred meters away, high above a scurry of russet-tiled roofs, soars the dome of the Medici Chapels and the bell tower of San Lorenzo church. We swing open the pair of tall windows and there, immediately to the right, is Florence's best-known symbol – Brunelleschi's dome – tethered to the cathedral like a hot air balloon that's ready to rise to Heaven. We have arrived at Via Roma 3, our home for the next nine months.

After a cursory look at the bedroom, kitchen, bathroom, and combination dressing and storage room, we walk up two flights of stairs to the rooftop terrace, shared with the building's other tenants. Signor Bianchi is so proud that he actually executes a pirouette while showing off the 360-degree view of the city punctuated by castellated towers and delicate spires. To the north, Signor Bianchi points out the ancient town of Fiesole on the hazy Tuscan hills, and to the south, San Miniato al Monte, home to Benedictine monks.

So close they seem within easy reach are Florence's three most famous structures: the eight-sided Baptistery built in the eleventh century, the Cattedrale di Santa Maria del Flore, better known as the Duomo, and Giotto's Campanile, the cathedral's slender bell tower. The early afternoon sun makes their marble façades of pink, white, and green glow as brightly as if they were in the final stages of being fired in a heavenly kiln.

Scaffolding blocks our view of the lantern – the architectural feature atop the Duomo, with windows, a golden orb, and cross. How much longer, I ask, will the restoration work continue? "*Infinito*," says Signor Bianchi. "As soon as they get around, they start all over again."

We could have stayed and gaped all day, but Signor Bianchi beckons us back to the apartment to inspect the gas cooktop, electric oven, dishwasher, fridge, clothes washer, and dryer. Of course, Signor Bianchi has no clue how to operate the appliances, although he does demonstrate how to start the central heating system – on November 1 – when the hordes of tourists and the oppressive 35°C heat of summer are long gone.

Signor Bianchi phones his daughter Francesca, and a few minutes later a beautiful young woman with curly black hair appears. At thirty and unmarried, Francesca still lives with her parents. No apartment freedom for her. "It is different for a woman in this country than in yours," she says with a shy smile that shows off deep dimples.

Despite her degree in civil engineering, Francesca knows nothing about any of the machinery. The next plea goes to Signor Bianchi's wife, Roberta. When she calls back, I realize his cell phone ring tone plays Verdi, the famous composer who lived in Florence and wrote operas including *Aida* and *La Traviata*. Roberta joins us but since she has not lived in this investment apartment, she has not operated these particular models. Still, she offers enough helpful generalities to get us going. Just as well there are no detailed explanations – our jet-lagged brains couldn't have retained very much anyway.

Finally, in a flurry of handshakes and assurances of instruction booklets for the appliances and another armchair for the living room, the three depart saying *arrivederla*, the most formal Italian version of good-bye. When we get to know them better, we might use the more familiar *arrivederci*. *Ciao* is only for friends.

After a day and a night of crowded airports and cramped aircraft, Sandy and I are alone at last. We hug, let out a few whoops of joy at our safe arrival, and walk again to the windows. In addition to the historic Medici Chapels and the Duomo, there is also a bright yellow construction crane towering over a restoration project. Our New World reaction would be exasperation at this modern intrusion. Here in the Old World, our response is somehow muted and more tolerant. We see the old buildings and the new equipment as a juxtaposition of our two selves. As a mature art student on a voyage of self-discovery and a business writer undergoing a transformation to cultural observer, we have joined the 7 million students, artists, and tourists who annually visit Florence, a city that flourished before Christopher Columbus set sail. Those medieval explorers looked for, among other things, the Fountain of Youth, when in fact the earthly form of life everlasting has been here all along because so much of the Renaissance beauty has been preserved.

In addition to the spectacular view, there is a constant buzz from the tourists in the streets below, but we realize that the noise will eventually die down at day's end. As for Giotto's Campanile, we wonder about the nighttime clamor from its eighteen bells, one of which is aptly named *Shrilla* or the Shrieker. We have a place to lay our heads, but we might not sleep.

❧

At 7 a.m. we are awakened by melodious pealing from the Campanile, accompanied a few minutes later by grace notes from San Lorenzo. After a transatlantic flight through six time

zones such a luxurious sleep-in is unusual. The tintinnabulation of bells is the best possible welcome; even the Shrieker – thankfully silent all night – sounds happy we're here.

Renting an apartment sight unseen was not our original plan. We looked at a number of websites, peered at thumbnail photos of interiors, and decided while it might be possible to rent via the Internet for a one-week holiday, we didn't want to lock ourselves in for a long-term stay. We planned to fly to Florence, stay in a bed and breakfast, and then visit available apartments to see precisely what we were getting. Then I panicked. After all, I don't go to Schenectady, N.Y., for an overnight without a reservation, why would we head to Italy for nine months without lining up a lease?

Heavy e-mail traffic ensued with Milligan & Milligan, the rental agency that seemed to have the widest choice. We asked questions about half a dozen places, but kept returning to the pictures of the apartment with the dome visible through the window, the one where the monthly rent was a hefty 2,200 euros. "You're only going to do this once," said Sandy's brother, Rob. "Don't go on the cheap." After some negotiations, we struck a deal at a still very expensive 1,930 euros a month, about C$3,000, for our "Room with a View."

On our first full day we explore the neighborhood, fill up the larder, and ogle fashion in the shop windows and on the busy sidewalks. Everything and everyone seems to radiate vibrant energy: the sun-drenched pavement, the glories of centuries past, and the hordes of happy people. In the evening we watch from our window as a group assembles near the

Baptistery, the oldest structure in Florence. At first they look like a ragtag bunch: a few musicians waiting for their mates, some elderly ladies with little else to do, and a gaggle of women with children in strollers. The group grows larger and we decide to go down and join the throng, which had by now become several hundred families. The children were carrying paper lanterns lit from within by candles, a most unlikely source of power in this day of Game Boys and iPods run by alkaline batteries and computer chips.

Rificolona, the Festival of the Lanterns, turns out to be the annual parade that coincides with the eve of the Feast of the Madonna. One young man in the crowd wears a t-shirt announcing: "Mary is my home girl." Above these words the virgin is portrayed in a modern-day charcoal sketch, the halo suggested by cartoon lines. She looks like Popeye's girlfriend Olive Oyl, the way Edvard Munch might have rendered her.

The lanterns, both store-bought and homemade, come in dozens of shapes and designs. There are animals – a cat, a dog with dangly ears, a colorful parrot, even Mickey Mouse. There's a house and several modes of transportation: an airplane, boat, and locomotive. Some lanterns have Japanese floral patterns or portray a four-tiered pagoda; others consist of rainbow stripes or abstract swoops. The most popular motif is a happy sunshine face with full ruby lips and long black lashes.

The festival had its origins in the seventeenth century when rural peasants carrying lanterns walked all night to the early-morning market outside Santissima Annunziata. That same basilica is our destination as we join the procession wending its way along Via Cavour, led by men pulling a giant lantern, accompanied by women dressed in peasant costume. All are serenaded by a marching band founded in 1842 that proudly carries the name of Giuseppe Verdi on its flag. The band members range in age, from a man of eighty on clarinet to a boy of ten who taps a snare drum but mostly watches. Some of the players carry another form of portable lantern, a book light sticking out of a breast pocket, so they can read the sheet music mounted on their instruments. No open flames for them.

What might normally have been a ten-minute walk becomes a one-hour promenade because of the swelling numbers and the sheer enjoyment of the event. Of all the parades in all the world, this must be one of the few that's held after dark and involves so many families, from infants in arms to grandparents with canes.

Most of the young boys carry peashooters that are half a meter long and have a gummy substance wrapped around the middle as if to supply a better two-handed grip on these mighty instruments that appear capable of great devastation. The warriors are supposed to wait until the end of the parade when, with permission, they can pepper holes in the lanterns, but some of them send their missiles flying early, a process that involves much mental math to plan the arc and gauge the distance. Their targets include a portly man in a doorway, a woman watching from a second-storey window, and unsuspecting friends walking ahead. This is the perfect boyhood prank because once the distant target feels the bite it's too late to spot the culprit who has hidden the heavy artillery and assumed an angelic pose.

The evening's overall feeling is communal and historic, festive and fun. As the parade pours into the piazza at Santissima Annunziata, the crowd on the steps making up three sides of the square applauds appreciatively. In place of the medieval market is a candyland carnival, with spun floss, roasted nuts, and other sugary treats. The boys are torn. Do they start their peashooter barrage in earnest or gobble the goodies? Most find a way to do both.

It's our second day here in this city of four hundred thousand and already we've marched with the locals. No better introduction and welcome could there be. We will never be Florentines, but we are shedding the usual tourist garb. A wooden platform in the middle of the piazza groans under the weight of serious-minded men in dark suits. As the dignitaries belly toward a line of microphones, and the speeches begin, we slip away. Why spoil a good thing?

Much of the first week is taken up getting our bearings. We walk everywhere and don't miss having a car at all because few destinations are farther than fifteen minutes away. Maps are helpful but some street names change every few blocks so you waste a lot of time trying to follow a carefully planned route. Best approach is simply to plunge ahead and see something different, rather than play it safe and travel the same route as yesterday. To complicate matters, each street has a double numbering system, so there are two fifteens, two eighty-eights, two everythings. Numbers listed in black are residences, red for businesses, but 55 and 55r (where *r* stands for *rosso*, red) aren't necessarily anywhere near each other. In fact, 53r may be nowhere near 55r. Rather than be a nuisance, it's a plus. If we can't find an address right away, we will eventually, thereby making Florence the city of second chances. With the Duomo as our guide, we can't get lost anyway. As long as we keep the red-tiled dome in sight bubbling above other buildings, we know the way home.

We quickly fall into the European habit of shopping daily for food; everything is so fresh from the nearby countryside. The iron-and-glass Central Market is a handy ten minutes away, but to get there we must run the narrow and noisy gauntlet of the city's famous leather market where many prices aren't marked, depending instead on the buyer's apparent capacity to pay. The Central Market is more organized, with fixed prices at dozens of permanent shops on two floors. They offer fruit and vegetables, fish and meat, olives and spices, mushrooms and nuts, cheese and wine. A small shark-like creature, displayed with a tiny fish in its mouth, must have been caught in the financial district.

Customers cannot handle the fruit or vegetables; the vendor does the choosing for you, so tourists tend to be sold the poor-quality items. We decide to buy at the same stalls each day in the hopes of being treated like regulars. In Italy, such links don't take long. On our second visit to one of the fruit and vegetable stands, a venerable man in his seventies gives Sandy a wide smile and adds a free peach to her selection. On the next visit he cups her face with his gnarled hands and whispers something in her ear that I'm sure is complimentary, if only I had been able to hear. To distract me from his flirtatious activities, he hands me half a nectarine. The red flesh is so ripe that I have to bend over to bite into it as juice drips down my chin onto the cement floor. Not since the temptation of Adam had a man so enjoyed a piece of fruit while something else happened that was beyond his ken. After Sandy's art classes began and I shopped alone, the vendor was far less attentive. There was neither free fruit nor friendly hands, so I went elsewhere with my market basket.

One day we range farther afield, looking for a supermarket behind the train station that's supposed to have a larger selection and lower prices. We never arrive. On our way through the station, among the milling passengers destined for Milan, Genoa, and Rome, we are besotted by a trio of performers on stilts. The faces of the two women and a man are painted white and flecked with gold, their smiles almost zen-like. They wear white silk blouses and black pants and walk on thin stilts that make them seem two storeys tall. Flowing from their arms are diaphanous pieces of silken material so that as they stride along they look like graceful giraffes disguised as dragonflies conducting an orchestra of awestruck observers that include us.

Accompanying the pageantry is the incongruous sound of a five-piece Dixieland band playing "When the Saints Go Marching In." Last time we heard a live version of that famous tune was in New Orleans, played by the Preservation Hall Jazz Band. There we sat on wooden bleachers and listened to them tootle beneath a hand-lettered sign that read: Requests $2;

When The Saints Go Marching In, $5. At the train station in Florence, this excellent rendition is free.

We spend so long enjoying the sights and sounds that we never find the phantom supermarket. We settle instead for a smaller grocery store with good prices, which include a bottle of Prosecco, a sparkling wine, for four euros. How does anyone get anything done in Florence? There's too much to see, even during a shopping trip.

◦⟨⟩◦

As we venture farther afield we discover that the fare of one euro per person each way on the #7 bus makes the twenty-minute ride to Fiesole among the best, and certainly cheapest, of the many day trips available in Florence. During the first half of the eight-kilometer ride the bus trundles through narrow city streets, but soon we are in a wooded area north of the city, and then we're climbing higher and higher, past magnificent villas partially hidden behind walls and hedges, all with views of the verdant valley below. Florence lies in a broad bowl surrounded by Tuscan hills that are old, wise, and worn down by the weather. During the span of a few hours we watch the hills change their clothing several times, from mist-shrouded in the early-morning fog to clearly visible with the sun glinting on the glass of far-off windows, then to blue-gray and bedecked with scudding puffs of white-cotton cloud. The Duomo – so large and looming from our apartment window – is but one note in the sprawling symphony of colors and shapes.

Fiesole is quiet and peaceful, the perfect place to think about the meaning of life. The Etruscans who settled here around 600 BC created a sophisticated society. Some of their stone walls still stand; their tiny statues are amazingly modern and show an understanding of anatomy as well as an eye for beauty. Offerings presented to their god, Minerva, include minuscule carved legs or a foot, votives representing whatever part of the body had been healed by her divine intervention. Sculptor Alberto Giacometti's sinuous bronze works must have been influenced by the Etruscans, his style is so similar.

The Roman army set up camp in the valley below, cut off supply routes, and easily conquered the Etruscans. The Romans built a temple on top of the Etruscan shrine and then added walkways, walls, columns, and a complicated water system for steam, a swimming pool, and hot and cold baths. A semicircular two-thousand-seat amphitheatre from the first century BC is still used for summer drama festivals. Recently, archeologists halted street repairs in Piazza Mino da Fiesole when more Roman ruins were discovered. In such a place, where the distant past is ever present, one might well ask: How best should you spend your brief time, your three score and ten?

We have a café lunch in the piazza, straining to see over the hoarding and into the construction site turned archeological dig where there is an unusual pair of equestrian statues. Equestrian subjects are my favorite statues and I've never before seen anything like this work that captures an encounter between two riders on horseback who meet, pause to speak, and are shown shaking hands. We also have just such an encounter when a man sits down at a nearby table and says hello to Sandy. She smiles, waves, and then notices his shirt, which reads Hamilton Health Services. "Are you really from Hamilton?" she asks.

He is joined by his wife and another Canadian couple who are also from Hamilton. When they learn we are living in Florence until next May, they sigh and say they want to move in with us. When the women hear Sandy is attending art school, they want to move into her life. Says one, "You're my hero." We had heard similar comments before leaving Toronto. We already knew that we had done the right thing by shaking up our lives to come here for a long stay, but this supplies further confirmation.

Later that day, back in Florence, we stroll to the Mercato Nuovo (New Market), an arcaded and covered space filled with stalls selling leather goods, rugs, pashmina scarves, and trinkets. The goods are not our goal. The Holy Grail is *Il Porcellino*. The word means "little pig," but this bronze statue is actually a wild boar about the size of a pony, lolling on his haunches, his mouth open in a wicked grin that allows a trickle of water to fall into a grate below.

According to tradition, those who rub *Il Porcellino* will enjoy good luck and a guaranteed return to Florence, so his snout has been polished to a high sheen by countless hands. As for those who have rubbed his ample penis, that protrusion being the only other body part that shines as brightly, I cannot say. All I know for sure is that returning to Florence is something we don't have to worry about. We're here, and we're staying for the next nine months.

September

OUR NEW LIFE IN FLORENCE had its beginnings in 2000 when Sandy's mother died after a lingering illness. Sandy had been the main caregiver for many months, so she needed something to fill the void and help her deal with her grief. Art had always tugged at the hem of her life, but there never seemed to be enough time to nourish her talent, except for a few sketches while on family holidays. Somewhere there's a pencil drawing of me lying nude on a cottage couch. The rendering was excellent but I'm more scrawny bird than Renaissance Man.

Sandy had taken some art lessons from Pat Fairhead, a noted watercolorist, who praised her natural talent but urged her to enroll at the Ontario College of Art and Design (OCAD) in order to improve her drawing skills. The week after her mother's funeral, Sandy presented herself at OCAD. Entrance standards are high – you don't just sign up and start classes. The rigorous process required five courses over two semesters followed by an appearance before a panel where Sandy's portfolio passed muster. She was admitted to the four-year drawing and painting program, which she planned to take over a more leisurely six or seven years. That way she could enjoy the journey, rather than just dash through to the destination of a degree.

I'd get regular reports on her fellow students, most in their late teens or early twenties, what hair color was popular, and the latest in body piercing or tattoos. Despite the difference in age, the other students readily accepted Sandy. The group creativity was celebratory as Sandy worked in oils, acrylics, charcoal, watercolor, and wire sculpture. In March 2004 she heard about a program in which a small group of OCAD students spend the fall and winter semesters in Florence. The application deadline, however, had just passed. Our daughter, Alison, who teaches art history at McMaster University, knows all about the vagaries of academe. "There are deadlines," she said, "and there are deadlines."

Sure enough, the deadline for studies in Florence had been extended. Sandy applied, wrote the required statement of artistic intent, and showed the selection committee half a dozen pieces of her work. From the many applicants, she was one of nineteen picked to attend the program that ran from September 2004 to April 2005.

For me, the timing was perfect. I was just completing my book about Edgar Bronfman Jr., *The Icarus Factor*, for publication in the fall so I was free to travel. As for September 2005, who knew? As someone who has written extensively about family businesses, I was curious about the celebrated success of

Italian artisans and family firms through many generations. We decided that the time was right for both of us to enjoy this fantasy adventure together.

Preparations would have been hectic enough, but there were unexpected calamities. In April Sandy fell and broke her right shoulder and in May she had an emergency appendectomy. As if that wasn't enough, we decided to sell our house, which involved a disruptive two-month-long process and sixty showings before we found our buyer. We parked the proceeds in the bank and put our furniture in storage.

Every time we faced what seemed like another insurmountable obstacle, one of us would buck up the other and say, "Yes, we're doing the right thing." We'd lived abroad before – in London, England, from 1987 to 1988 and in Washington, D.C., from 1989 to 1993 – so we knew how difficult and demanding, as well as enriching and rewarding, such foreign sojourns could be. We had moved in the past because of my work, but this was different. Florence would be Sandy's time.

Among the many reasons we decided to stir up our lives were the feelings that we had become possessed by our possessions, that it was time to cast off some material items and travel more lightly. As high school sweethearts, married for almost forty years, we're on the leading edge of the baby boomers. We had watched too many friends and acquaintances retire into a comfy life of golf and bridge and drinking.

Worse, some were dying. Bob and Heather, our oldest friends as a couple, went on a cruise in the Gulf of Mexico. Two days out, Bob suffered a heart attack. He was airlifted to New

Orleans but died in hospital before they could operate. He was sixty. One of the last things we did before leaving Canada was to attend Bob's funeral in Ancaster, Ontario. "Florence," announced Sandy, "is the now or never plan."

◇⋈◇

Sandy's idea of taking new living space and turning it into a home means we spend the first afternoon rearranging the furniture. "I can see it done," she keeps saying, but it takes some doing. The previous tenants had used the foyer as a sitting area so the TV and a two-seater couch were crammed together inside the front door. The living room had served as a second bedroom with a pair of single beds jumbled together with chairs. We moved everything that was in the foyer into the living room, took one of the beds apart, hid the pieces in the storage room, and set up the other as a daybed along the wall in the now empty foyer. The final struggle was to slide and tilt a tall bookcase through the living-room door into the foyer so the unit would be available to hold what we needed on our daily rounds: maps, guides, notebooks, sketchbooks, and a small backpack for my laptop on the regular visits to the Internet café to send e-mails and check for news from home.

As a result, we now have a one-bedroom apartment. The foyer can breathe and the living room looks normal, with a couch, chairs, TV, and a leather-topped library table at the window where I can write. A seventeenth-century armoire, thankfully too heavy to move, remains rooted where it was to hold coats. On either side of the armoire are two antique chairs with tall backs, splayed legs, and feral feet that look as if they were carved by and for gnomes. We await their arrival and explanation.

The bedroom, with the same splendid views as the living room, requires no reorganizing of its queen-sized bed, night tables, dresser, and Art Nouveau floor lamp, which looks like an exotic ivy with golden leaves. Sandy sets up a trestle table and easel to paint at the window with its excellent northern light. The ceilings in all the rooms are three meters high, the walls white, and the windows large so the overall feeling is luminous and light-hearted.

We spend a lot of time at the windows, pinching ourselves to see if we're really here, taking in the scene that includes a window nearby with an artist's easel visible, an observatory dome on top of a house, a stray cat gingerly walking along a rooftop ridge, a row of chimney pots that must have been hand-made because each looks slightly different, and a woman watering a rooftop garden. Even the advertising is suited to the surroundings. The sole visible billboard displays a Martini logo that lights up at night in red and yellow neon.

Sometimes we just stand and close our eyes at the open windows, feeling the gentle breezes and listening to the buzz from below, the screel of chimney swifts whizzing by, the resonant church bells, the whistle of a worker, the rise-and-fall siren of an ambulance, always with one ear cocked for something unusual like a new musician in the piazza or the thumping drum of an approaching parade.

We keep our windows open in spite of warnings that the

Florentine mosquito is like nothing we'd ever experienced, even in the deep woods of Canada. Because we're not accustomed to their particular brand of poison, everyone told us that we'd swell up like red puffballs at first nibble. We dutifully visited IKEA before leaving Canada and bought a long tube of mosquito netting attached to a plastic circle meant to be suspended above the bed. We'd sleep inside the tent created and be safe from certain death.

Except there's a ceiling fan and we never could figure out how to suspend the contraption so that the netting didn't become a knotted mess amid the rotating blades. No matter, local stores are full of other devices to do battle against the foe. We bought a plug-in instrument that sits on the floor and looks like the red dome light on a police car. Inside there's a potion that infuses the room with fatal fumes that somehow slay pests but not people. So far, so good; we haven't seen a single skeeter. And the killer device is not even plugged in.

The ceramic floors in the foyer, hall, and bathroom date from 1929, when the building was erected, and were said to be made by some world-famous company that's no longer in business, the name of which no one can remember. All I know is that it took three mornings on my hands and knees to scrub away the grime that had built up on the world-famous bathroom tile. How ironic, I thought: all those European women who moved to Canada and then cleaned house for a living, and here I was in Italy doing the same. Without pay. But when I was finished, the beautiful floral motif was far more visible than before.

Every afternoon the mellifluous sounds of someone playing

a piano come wafting through our kitchen window, which looks onto a sun-filled interior quadrangle where laundry hangs from a variety of clotheslines suspended outside the windows. Across the way and one floor up live two young women, one with black hair, the other blond. Sandy saw the blond step from the shower to dry herself with a white towel and baptized her Fatima. My sightings were limited to more mundane moments like watching her wash dishes wearing yellow gloves.

In addition to the view of such flitting apparitions, our kitchen has a small table with three chairs, a fridge much larger than the usual European variety, and a washing machine called Candy that can knock the bejeebers out of the most durable fabric. The gas-fired cooking elements don't work. There's spark and there's gas, but the elements won't stay lit. The only way to make coffee is to press the igniter then hold the gas dial for the required five minutes of brewing time, otherwise the gas goes out. Signor Bianchi assures us that a technician will come, maybe as early as next week. "*Dio spero*," he adds, laughing and looking Heavenward for help. I hope so, too, and join him in prayer with my singed fingers.

❧

Firenze, as the Italians call this medieval city in the middle of the Italian peninsula, is the capital of Tuscany. Founded in 59 BC by the Romans, this has been a place of politics and intrigue since the thirteenth century when the Guelphs – city dwellers, artisans, and merchants who supported the pope – fought for control with the Ghibellines, feudal nobility who favored the

Holy Roman Empire. The Guelphs won and dominated local government.

There were German Guelphs, too. Sandy and I grew up in Guelph, an hour west of Toronto. When John Galt founded the city in 1827 he gave it the German surname of the British Royal family. After the First World War broke out, the Royals changed their name to Windsor, but Guelph continued to call itself the Royal City. When we lived in Guelph there was a large Italian population that had emigrated after the Second World War. About 20 per cent of the city's thirty thousand residents had Italian roots, so we had school friends from the second generation: Valenti, Balconi, Tersigni, and de Corso. In Florence, we feel right at home.

Starting early in the fifteenth century, the Medici banking family ruled Florence, with some interruptions, until 1737. The dynasty produced two popes and, along with the Church, were patrons to sculptors, painters, and architects. In the film *The Third Man*, Harry Lime aptly captures the creative output of those times when he says: "In Italy for thirty years under the Borgias they had warfare, terror, murder, and bloodshed, but they produced Michelangelo, Leonardo da Vinci, and the Renaissance. In Switzerland, they had brotherly love, five hundred years of democracy and peace, and what did they produce? The cuckoo clock."

According to UNESCO, 60 per cent of the world's art is in Italy, and 60 per cent of that is found in Tuscany. I'll do the math: more than one-third of the world's art can be found in Florence or within an easy two-hour drive.

Other famous Florentines include Dante, who took the Tuscan language and made it the national tongue, and Leon Battista Alberti, who developed art criticism. Lorenzo Ghiberti was the first artist to write his autobiography, Filippo Brunelleschi was the father of modern architecture, Leonardo da Vinci was the quintessential Renaissance man, and Giorgio Vasari was the creator of art history.

Vasari's successor is Frederick Hartt, the modern era's most highly regarded expert in Renaissance art. "The country roads are still traveled, and the hill farms still worked, by pairs of colossal and surprisingly gentle long-horned oxen," wrote Hartt about Tuscany. "The smoke still rises from the ancient towns on their hilltops. And views across the lines of cypresses and up the rocky ledges still reveal what might be the background of a fresco by Benozzo Gozzoli. It is the hard-won harmony between man and nature that makes not only the landscape of Italy but also the art of its people different from any other in the world."

Before the harmony, however, there were feisty young rebels. The artist Masaccio was only twenty-six in 1427 when *The Trinity*, the first artwork to use perspective, was unveiled in Santa Maria Novella. Other painters were still following the flat, more stylized manner that had been around since the Middle Ages. *The Trinity* was so different that people lined up by the thousands outside the church to admire his work.

The arresting artistry of shop windows filled with androgynous mannequins in a nonchalant slouch performs the same eye-catching function today. Incongruous combinations include denim, wool check, and tulle – all used on one outfit. Satin and chain are stitched together with leather and pearl. Silk camisoles and skimpy skirts are combined with knee-high leather boots of huge proportions. Fur coats and wool dresses are turned inside out, the skins and seams showing. The styles are so out of sync with anything we'd ever seen before that they seem like a response to terrorism. Since 9/11, the enemy resides within, so designers and artists reveal those formerly hidden interior spaces.

One of the delights of living in our apartment building is that we can ride down the elevator, walk out the front door, and plunge immediately into the frenetic sights and sounds of Via Roma. Although the surrounding several blocks are supposed to be for pedestrians, the traffic is constant: horse-drawn carriages with drivers clearing the way using klaxon horns, taxis traveling too quickly, trucks sweeping debris left by tourists – and most dangerous of all – the deadly bicycle. You quickly learn never to change direction without first checking over your shoulder for the stealthy two-wheelers on silent rubber tires.

Fifteen steps from our door is the postcard view of the Duomo, the one where tourists take pictures of each other with the backdrop of the Baptistery on the left, the Duomo in the middle, and the Campanile on the right. Once a year during the Renaissance, Florentines brought all the babies born during the previous twelve months to the Baptistery. As each baby received the sacrament, a white bean was set aside for a girl, a black bean for a boy, so population growth could be calculated at the end of the day.

Begun in 1296, construction of the Duomo took 150 years, using local marble: white from Carrara, green from Prato, and pink from Siena. The Gothic façade, a nineteenth-century addition, is a busy collection of busts, statuary, mosaics, and rose windows. As with the Tuscan hills, the Duomo looks different in different lights. In the morning, the backlit Duomo is brooding and pensive. The early afternoon sun renders the colors so bright you shield your eyes as the gold glisters on the mosaics, while in the evening everything softens to a jade and apricot glow. Brunelleschi's dome goes through a similar transformation and at various points in the day can be brown, orange, or red. Every time we pass, we stop, stare, and see new elements that make us wonder where our eyes had been only an hour before.

The numerous beggars are an obvious urban problem, but, unlike the lethargic homeless of North America, even the streetpeople here provide a form of performance art. Long-skirted and sulky gypsies shake their plastic cups; a spastic man with beseeching eyes wobbles about on crutches; a boy-like waif kneels in prayer with supplicant hands holding a few pennies; an older man removes his leg prostheses and places them beside him in order to show he is the victim of something unspeakable; young Goths with morose dogs play penny whistles and display hand-lettered signs pleading for help from hunger.

And yet. And yet. Walk around another corner, and there will be a busker playing an accordion, harmonica, piccolo, or musical saw. Once there was even a bagpiper looking somewhat out of place. There might be a school choir on tour giving an impromptu performance, or a soloist with a cello, violin, or saxophone. One pan piper performs with a synthesizer and so many speakers that he sounds like an entire troupe. He has not just one collection plate, but two, so costly are his accoutrements. On another occasion there was an improbable foursome of Peruvians dressed like North American Indians in fringed jackets, buckskin leggings, and feather headdresses.

A short two-minute stroll away is Piazza della Repubblica, the largest public space in Florence, where there is always music from a rotating series of individual performers and groups such as the five Romanians who call themselves Gypsy Show. One of them hammers on the strings of an open-topped zither as if it were a xylophone while his colleagues play violin, bass, accordion, and guitar. A string quartet offers selections from Vivaldi's *Four Seasons*. There are also solo performers: a Russian soprano with a headset microphone, and two classical guitarists, both with serious miens in keeping with their music. They seem to have a pact that means only one of them plays at a time. If a guitarist is strumming, the next musician to arrive waits while the first finishes an hour-long set.

One time we got entangled among a group of twelve lively players marching with such a quickstep shuffle that their legs looked like slide trombones. The pace at which they passed meant that you couldn't make a monetary contribution even if you wanted to. I think the name of the group was the Fantastix, but they went by so fast, I can't be sure. There are always jugglers, spray-paint artists, and costumed personages who hold a pose and only move when a passerby donates a coin. Among this particular genre there is a Roman centurion, a pair of philosophers who conduct mock debate in mime, and a white-robed figure with Medusa-like hair. If the timing were right, you could watch the performers sitting on the curb, putting on their makeup, and getting dressed. For gamblers, there was often a shell game up a side street. After a while, I knew who the shill was and could correctly guess, along with him, the location of the pea under one of the three matchboxes. When the shill won, the choice was always obvious. Every other time all bettors lost their fifty-euro note with amazing speed. I neither won nor lost because I wisely never played.

As if all that weren't enough, there were daily protest parades by peaceniks, union members, students, skinheads, or the middle class. One group of two hundred marchers, led by a black-robed figure of death carrying a scythe, complained about the methods of child psychiatrists who prescribe electric shock treatments, not the most likely of campaigns. All such demonstrations were carefully monitored with half a dozen police officers walking fore and aft in a manner that both gave legitimacy to the cause and comfort to passersby.

Apart from performing parade duty, the police are an active presence in the central historic district because the Duomo, the treasures of the Uffizi Galley, and Piazza della Signoria, home to the city government, are all within a five-minute walk of each other. The three levels of uniformed officers who patrol the pedestrian area on foot, horseback, and by car include the municipal police, the haughty carabinieri, and from time to time, heavily armed swat-teams of soldiers that appear so suddenly with their hulking Humvees that you wonder if you'd missed the announcement of a terrorist alert.

Other than reassuring visitors, the main occupation of the constabulary is to harass the street vendors. Various ethnic groups, none with work permits, control specific commodities. Asian men sell exotic birds and grasshoppers woven out of leaves or they paint the buyer's name in colorful script on a long sheet of paper. Asian women stalk pedestrians while shaking colorful scarves in outstretched hands. Pakistanis peddle roses to restaurant patrons. Young men from Senegal and the Ivory Coast sell counterfeit brand-name watches, handbags, CDs, and sunglasses.

When a vendor spots police approaching, he whistles. At the signal, other sellers sweep their goods into their blankets and toss the bagged items over their shoulder. Those with cardboard stands collapse the display, hiding the items safely inside what is now a carrier. The Asian vendors scatter from sight, while the Africans are more likely to loll against a wall, or peer innocently down a side street as if wondering the whereabouts of some friend who promised to show up. The police, satisfied to have at least disrupted the retail process, pass nonchalantly by, paying no attention to the ridiculous charade. As soon as the officers are ten steps away, business resumes. If caught in the act, fines or deportation are rare, but goods can be seized. I only witnessed the aftermath of one such bust when a man wearing a suit, who had obviously been summoned by the sellers, was arguing with police about what would happen next.

The official symbol of Florence is a white fleur-de-lys on a red background, but it should really be The Lost Couple, a man and a woman at an intersection peering at a flapping paper map and then staring up quizzically at the street signs all the while arguing about what direction they should take for Ponte Vecchio and the Arno River. Many a marriage has been sorely tested because no cartographer has been able to accurately capture the twists and turns of real life. One man I saw carried a pocket compass. Who would want to travel with him?

Since the early-morning train bombings in Madrid in March 2004, when almost two hundred commuters were killed and two thousand were injured, al-Qaeda has been widely expected to strike Italy. Like Spain, Italy was a member of the U.S.-led coalition of the willing that attacked Iraq in 2003. Florence, Rome, and Venice have been specifically added to al-Qaeda's list of prime targets, because of the number of U.S. visitors and ex-pats here, not to mention the symbolism of Muslims striking at so much Christian art.

Terrorism has certainly changed the lives of the five thousand American students in Florence who attend programs sponsored by several dozen colleges: Sarah Lawrence, New York University, Gonzaga, Kent State, and Syracuse, among others. School entrances once open to anyone are now locked tight and monitored by video cameras. St. James, the American Church, herds every arriving sinner through a narrow gate in a high wrought-iron fence so everyone can be scrutinized by a church employee sometimes aided by an armed security guard.

Several American students have been kidnapped and held

for ransom; one was killed. Since terrorists can't tell the difference between a Canadian and an American, those who live here full-time warn us to be quiet and unassuming. Don't speak English in a loud voice or draw attention to yourself, they say. As guises go, that's easy. Aren't these our national traits?

Of the nineteen students in the OCAD program, most are in their early twenties. Four men live together in an apartment; five women share a house; others pair off or live alone. A bicycle left behind by a member of last year's class is raffled off. Payment for the prize, which came complete with helmet, lock, and chain, is to send the donor, now back home in Toronto, some of the Italian coffee he knew he would sorely miss.

The studios, near the train station on Via Nazionale, are Sandy's second home. The students share the two-floor space, as many as four to a large room, each room with tall windows. Projects are self-directed but must receive advance approval from the program coordinator for the fall term, Laura Millard. Attendance is mandatory three days a week; the other two days are free for inspiration and creativity elsewhere. On those days Sandy and I often work together in our separate apartment spaces, conscious that interruptions could halt creativity.

OCAD's part-time art history professor, Peter Porçal, who has lived in Florence for thirty years, reveals the glories of the Renaissance through three-hour walks and lectures every Wednesday morning. Being the only spouse attached to the group, I was able to join the outings. Peter's introductory lecture includes a lyrical reverie about what draws artists to Florence. The light of northern Italy is silvery and sharp – it makes one squint. In Florence, the light is sweet, soft, and diffused. We listen while he talks about Greek myths and realize our education was sadly neglected. We also learn that Donatello and Michelangelo were both gay, a hint of the revelations to come.

Daily life begins for me at 4 a.m. when I get up to write, a habit I acquired more than twenty years ago when I had a day job. Since the early 1980s I've always had a book on the go. The first round of bells from Giotto's Campanile awaken Sandy at 7 a.m. for breakfast of muesli, yoghurt, fresh fruit, and coffee. The bells of San Lorenzo join in at ten to eight so we are always well serenaded. During the rest of day, the bells remain mostly silent, coming to life again between 5:30 p.m. and 7 p.m. On Sundays the jubilant pealing announces services throughout the day. There isn't a time we don't stop whatever we are doing to listen and marvel at the melodic sound.

The technician repairs our stove elements and we learn how to press down on the igniter with one hand, turn on the gas dial for six seconds with the other hand, and then give the dial a quick downward push and release. Like all else in this world, it's simple once you know how. We celebrate by making minestrone soup, with tomato, garlic, onions, celery, fennel, peas, beans, carrots, and pasta, that's hearty enough for a main course after a starter of melon and prosciutto. Even better, there's enough for another meal.

Food quickly becomes an integral part of the day: plan a

menu, choose the constituent parts, trundle them home in the bundle buggy we bought for twenty euros, prepare them, and finally, the triumph of eating, followed by washing up. Meals in Italy take longer to consume. In Toronto, a fridge full of items bought at the supermarket yielded a week of dinners, each gulped in twenty minutes. Here, all meals take an hour to eat because you talk about the taste, the feel of it in your mouth, the name in Italian, and the newly discovered shop where something came from. Pasta Fresca, a stall at the north end of the central market where the local restaurants buy their pasta, offers ten types of fresh pasta as well as half a dozen tasty sauces. Dinner for two takes no time at all to prepare and costs about six euros.

We share in the food preparation and clean up, but I do most of the shopping. With each outing I learn the name of a new vegetable, spice, or bread. There is a minor breakthrough on Day Seven when a vendor says *due quaranta* and I not only know exactly how much money he wants but readily pick out the correct coins from the handful in my pocket. One day, however, I try to buy a type of crusty bread called *salato*. Unlike most Tuscan breads, this one contains salt, a regular ingredient we're used to in Canada. I'd bought the bread before, but this time I mistakenly called it *saluto*. After much laughter and military salutes, they give me what I want. Through trial and error, we discover the best shops for various foodstuffs. Two blocks north for the well-priced wines; ten minutes east for cream-filled desserts; three streets down for a slice of focaccia, still warm from the oven and dripping with tomatoes and mozzarella cheese for a stand-up lunch at the counter; down that cul-de-sac for grapes with a hint of honey and two ripe melons – one ready to be eaten tonight and another for *domani*.

Prices are reasonable. In euros a clutch of fresh parsley is 60 cents, a fragrant fennel bulb costs 40 cents, four delicate slices of prosciutto are 1.15, a two-fisted bottle of Moretti beer, 1.35, the aforementioned *salato*, 1.45; a football-sized melon, a kilo of carrots, two heads of romaine, and four bananas, come to 4.35. The total was less than C$15 and means visiting six different vendors, but that's part of the joy. The non-food add-ons are expensive: two rolls of film cost 14 euros; a metal vessel called a *scalda latte*, to heat the milk for morning coffee, 6 euros; a new tea towel, 6 euros haggled down from 9.

Sandy is on a different sort of sensory overload as inspiration flows from Renaissance art and architecture, shop windows, fashion in the streets, high blue skies, and the Tuscan hills that change color hourly, from deep purple to dusky gray then light green followed by hazy blue. Sandy becomes a skilled street forager after discovering that discarded shoeboxes can hold art supplies. A two-meter piece of plastic venting for a clothes dryer is dragged home, washed in the bathtub, and then stacked alongside her growing collection of found objects: buttons, bottle caps, packing material, bits of squashed metal, and a paper party hat. In addition to using mixed media, Sandy also works in acrylic on nylon and canvas, watercolor on paper, and wire sculpture – for necklaces, bangles, and dresses.

After dinner, I bag up the garbage and leave it on the sidewalk for the 9 p.m. nightly pickup. There's no recycling;

everything goes out the door together. I do, however, find my own ecological way of foraging. We have too few clothes hangers so, after hunting high and low, I finally find a dozen for eight euros. Not a bad price, but that was all they had. I'd already been to several other stores with no hangers, and we needed a few more.

One night, as I put out the trash, a revelation occurs. Shops in our neighborhood must also be throwing away their unwanted items, so I went on a scavenger hunt and found hangers in all shapes and sizes. In other circumstances, such activity might be called garbage-picking but we preferred to call it gleaning, like peasants of old going through a field after the harvest, gathering the kernels of grain that had been left behind by the threshers. So there I was, amid the tourists heading out for dinner, sifting through trash bags and tossed-out boxes so our closets could feature the hangers of Valentino, Cavalli, Pucci, and Armani, all scrubbed clean, of course.

Day's end also includes a regular trip to the rooftop terrace, sometimes two. The first at 7:30 p.m. is to watch the setting sun create a riotous palette of colors that light up the clouds: red, pink, purple, mauve, orange, and one hue I swear was heliotrope. The second trip comes at 9:15 p.m. to watch what appear to be lamps in the tower atop the Palazzo Vecchio, huge guttering flames in the ramparts above Piazza della Signoria. I never learned why they were there and a couple of weeks later the flames were gone so we were happy to have seen them at all. And so to bed about 10 p.m., the street noise below fading away as we nod off, astonished to be here.

✳

Antonio Belvedere belongs to one of the noblest professions in Florence. He is a waiter. For the last year he has worked at Ristorante Paoli on Via dei Tavolini, a former chapel dating from the fourteenth century, with vaulted ceilings, frescoes of local scenes, and a row of ceramic tiles that runs above the wood wainscoting right around the restaurant. The tints in the 10 x 10 cm hundred-year-old tiles with crests of Tuscan towns were created from flowers and other natural sources. None of the plaques are identified but my favorite features two white mice, one running up each side of a cross. Opened in 1824, Paoli has attracted many famous clients. The visit of Woodrow Wilson in 1919 was commemorated with his bust set in a niche high on the wall. In modern times, Barbara Bush and Madonna have also dined here.

While he works, Antonio happily hums popular opera tunes and urges patrons to experiment, not just to eat the food they know. With Antonio, you order a salad just to see him select ingredients from the cart, then prepare and toss everything at tableside. In addition to Italian, Antonio is also fluent in English and French. He knows some Spanish and German, even a little Japanese, enough to explain the items on the menu and deliver such important phrases as "Would you like to share a plate?" – something the Japanese like to do.

After our encounter with Antonio, I was curious to learn more about him and his work so he agreed to meet me a few days later for a drink at a nearby café. His lunch shift over, he had a few hours off before dinner, so had changed from his white waiter's coat and black pants into street clothes: short-sleeved shirt, khaki pants, and light jacket. Born in the nearby town of Pistóia, Antonio is thirty-eight and has been working in restaurants since he was fifteen. At seventeen, he moved to Florence for a job in a pizzeria where they served one thousand walk-ins a day. He has also been a chef, but he has mostly worked as a waiter because he prefers the customer contact. He has an open face with an ever-present smile and soft brown eyes on the alert as if he's looking to foresee a need before the request forms in a patron's mind.

When Antonio applied to Paoli, he offered them his printed CV. "We don't want to see paper," was the reply. "We want to see you." He was hired after they watched him ply his craft. Such treatment was fine with him. "I want respect when I go to work. If you don't respect me, bye-bye."

At Paoli, called "the most characteristic restaurant in Florence" by Antonio, each waiter looks after eight tables and, in the busy season from April to October those tables can turn over twice in an evening. The regular menu is extensive and there are usually ten specials to explain. "It's not an easy restaurant," he said. "You need experience to work here." Of all the nationalities he serves, he by far prefers Americans. "Americans are number one. They're very kind and very easy. People say they talk too loud but they talk loud because they are happy people." For him, the Spanish are the most boisterous; the French the most sophisticated. He likes Canadians, too, and has an uncle in Edmonton but has never visited.

Paoli is among a small number of restaurants in Florence where waiters share in the day's revenue under a system known as *percentuale*. The staff meets every morning to divvy up 12 per cent of the previous day's proceeds, including the tips added to credit cards. As a result, everyone has an interest in how well their colleagues perform. "We take care of our jobs. The more people who come, the more we get." Antonio's share of that daily split yields about twenty-two hundred euros a month. At the end of each month, however, he pays income tax of 36 per cent on that amount. Tips handed to him directly in cash are another matter. "The government knows we get tips but says nothing. If we paid tax for tips, I'd change jobs."

When I asked him what he likes least about his job he can name nothing. "I love my job. It's inside me; it's the contact with the customers, the feeling." Moreover, there is the locale. "What's not to like in Florence? Florence is a very romantic town. People say Rome for the biggest, Florence for the beauty. Everybody in the world loves Tuscany, the views, the food, the wine. It's a very lucky place." He does not worry about the future, preferring to let events unfold as they will. "I never make plans. I'm a waiter, I can work anywhere in the world."

As our interview ends, and the bill arrives for our drinks, I ask him, as the expert in these matters, how much I should tip. Rather than reply directly, he tells a story about a recent restaurant meal he ate. The service was poor, but he left a two-euro tip anyway. "We are in the system," he says. As he speaks, he smiles and brushes his palms together three or four times in one of those gestures that, to me, means one hand washes the other.

Antonio nods at our waiter. "You can leave a tip if you like," then whispers, "He's Egyptian." "How do you know?" I ask. He places the end of his forefinger at the corner of his left eye and says, "In Florence, we know everybody."

With that, Antonio leaves. As I wait to pay the bill, I set aside a two-euro coin for a tip. Then I overhear a conversation, three tables away, between the Egyptian and a woman who'd had a drink alone. "I gave you a twenty," she says sharply. He feigns surprise and then adds a ten-euro note to her change. This is not the honorable system in which Antonio works. I pay the bill, palm my coin, and leave no tip.

As I head home and round the corner onto Via dei Calzaiuoli, who do I see rambling along with a large Dolce & Gabbana shopping bag, but Robin Williams. The movie star is shorter than I'd imagined, about 5 feet 9 inches, his slight frame made more bulky by a blue nylon jacket and baggy camouflage pants. Despite dark glasses and a stubble beard, he is readily recognizable.

Williams's manner, as he walks slowly along the fashionable pedestrian area past Furla and other fine shops, is fascinating. His gaze is fixed on the pavement about two meters ahead. He is smirking, as if trying out new lines in his mind and finding them very funny, indeed. While he might not have been avidly seeking the pleasure of fan recognition, he is delighted to be acknowledged. When a young couple with a baby ask to take his picture, he nestles beside the woman, puts an arm around her waist, and grins for the camera as her husband nervously lines up the shot. Then off he saunters, stopping to stare intently into a shop window until another couple spot him, speak, and they exchange pleasantries. He causes quite a stir in his wake as people realize who just passed. A female clerk from a shop called Pianegonda spies him, pulls a colleague out into the street, and points excitedly at his back.

Baudelaire called such a man a *flâneur* – someone who walks the streets with no specific plan except to see, be seen, and test the reaction of the populace. The daily question that confronts celebrities is this: Do I still enjoy fame or have I begun to fade? Comics are particularly needy and have a psyche even more fragile than most stars. Unlike stage actors who receive applause when a three-act play is over, comedians need immediate laughter after every punch line in their stand-up routine in order to be certain that they are loved. As a result Robin Williams is careful not to make eye contact – just in case the stranger does not know who he is or worse, realizes he's famous, but can't remember his name. If recognized, however, he responds. It is a nice difference that both protects his ego and produces constant adulation.

When I reach Via Roma 3, our concierge, Riccardo Gianotti, is standing in the doorway. Riccardo, who is in his thirties, has lived in Florence all his life and still cannot believe how many beautiful women there are locally. That's why he regularly leaves his seat in the glass booth inside the foyer to go outside, smoke a cigarette, and admire the view. "*Anche l'occhio vuole la sua parte,*" he says, which means, "The eye also wants his part." This was an afternoon for eyes: Antonio's eye on the Egyptian,

Robin Williams's eye on his status, and Riccardo's eye on the passing pulchritude.

❖

Our first month in Florence ends with a visit to a walled garden at the Palazzo Vivarelli Colonna. In a frenetic city of noisy motorbikes and a babel of languages, this garden is an oasis of calm. Open only two days a week, the garden is about to close until April; we are the only visitors on the last day of the season.

We walk through the gate and up a slight rise, feeling ourselves slowly being elevated into a state of rapture in this small but special place. The main feature is a wall sculpture in the form of a grotto, a sea cave viewed from within, with a background of blue sky and crashing ocean waves. Around the grotto are three figures, one playing the lyre plus two Pan-like creatures with cloven hooves that form the columns on either side to carry the arch that crowns the scene. In the tradition of such grottos, materials include coral and seashells of several sizes.

The grounds have pebbled walkways and a central fountain that feature a swan with a writhing snake in its mouth. Among the flowerbeds of seasonal blooms only the purple asters remain. Other plantings, laid out in careful patterns, include boxwood hedges as well as orange and lemon trees laden with fruit. Atop the high walls around the garden are stately urns, languid lions, and smiling cherubs. Specimen trees of olive, pine, and magnolia grandiflora tower over all else.

Neither war nor political wrangling, terrorism nor urban

problems are permitted to pass through these gates. Here, within the walls, dwell peace and tranquility. We sit holding hands on one of the stone benches, counting our myriad blessings. We have been living in Florence for a month and have everywhere been welcomed by a happy and generous people. We have reveled in the city's beauty and are beginning to learn a bit about the history all around us. In this storied environment, with creativity that ranges from Renaissance art and architecture to modern-day design in street fashion and shop windows, we are well launched on another important journey of discovery: the rebirth and renewal of our inner selves.

OCTOBER

FALL ARRIVES IN THE FORM of the Right Honorable Jean Chrétien walking alone along Via Roma at 2:30 p.m. on the first day of October. The former prime minister of Canada looks positively autumnal, like a transplanted piece of the Laurentian Shield, in greens and browns with a sweater casually draped over his shoulders in the European style. Even the purchases he carries, two gold shopping bags from Tod's, the Italian leather goods store, seem in keeping with the season.

Because he sees us grinning at him, he assumes we are Canadian and greets us like the seasoned campaigner he is. As we shake hands he quickly explains that the purchases do not belong to him, but to his wife and daughter who handed him the bags so they'd be free to browse and buy in other stores. "Now I am a servant," he says, then laughs and adds, "All my life I have been a public servant."

Along with their son-in-law, the Chrétiens are among forty from Canada attending the wedding of a nephew in Pisa the next day. While his wife and daughter shop, Chrétien had been swimming about in a warm bath of personal acknowledgment. At the corner, he'd had his picture taken with a group from Vancouver. Over by the Duomo he'd met people from his hometown. "I say hello, and shake hands, but I'm not campaigning for anything." The realization almost seems like a relief.

His new life of corporate boards and international representation sits lightly upon him. Revelations at the Gomery Inquiry about political payoffs in Quebec are in the future, so gone are the furrowed brow, the darting eyes, and the agitated look around the mouth so familiar when he was in power. The petty politics of Ottawa matter not a whit to us in Florence, or to him. He looks relaxed, prosperous, and at ease. However his legacy will be viewed by historians, this is a man content with his lot, comfortable in his own skin and satisfied with what he accomplished in life.

George W. Bush could not have taken that same agreeable constitutional on these streets. He would have been torn limb from limb by the locals and fed to a flock of pigeons. Neither he nor his foreign policies are popular. Go into any neighborhood square, look up at the apartments, and you'll see hanging from the windows numerous rectangular, rainbow-colored banners bearing one word: *Pace*. A year ago, when anti-Iraq feelings were at their peak, almost everyone displayed the Peace banner and there was a waiting list of buyers. One of the largest anti-war protests in the world took place in Florence when an estimated four hundred and fifty thousand marched, a gathering greater than the local population.

Peace is the pursuit of a somber row of seven women dressed in black who carry placards and often stand silently of an evening behind the Baptistery, representing views not uncommon in Italy. Two aid workers, both twenty-nine and both named Simona – Simona Pari and Simona Toretta – were captured by terrorists and held hostage in Iraq for three weeks in September. Known as *Le Simone* (the Simonas), they became national heroines – not just for their resolve while in captivity and safe release – but also for their stance after the incident. One of them, who had worked in Iraq for years, said she wanted to return but would not do so as long as U.S. troops remain. The Simonas are featured on television news, night after night, long after they have anything new to say: footage of them getting into cars, waving from balconies, just going about their normal business. Viewers can't seem to get enough of these two young Italian women who symbolize a widely held anti-American view.

And yet Florence depends upon the constant flow of American tourist dollars, a love-hate relationship with which Canadians will be all too familiar. We happily do business with Americans but dislike their bully-boy tactics when it comes to trade. The British hold similar anti-American views despite the so-called special relationship between the two countries. When we lived in England, people regularly mistook us for Americans, until they learned we were Canadians and would grow slightly warmer toward us colonials. Sandy once asked a curmudgeonly fishmonger in Hastings who was complaining about Americans just what the root cause was. "They took all our women during the war," he lamented. We did not tell him that Canadian troops brought home forty thousand war brides to twenty-six thousand for the Yanks. After a while, because the anti-Americanism in Britain seemed so irrational, we often would defend our Southern cousins. We do not do so in Italy; most Canadians would agree with the Italian stance.

Since 9/11, the number of American tourists is down dramatically. Visitors from Germany, France, Britain, and Austria account for 56 per cent of the tourist dollar, with Germans the most numerous. The Italians and the Germans, one-time war allies, have an interesting relationship. The Germans love the Italians but don't respect them. The Italians respect the Germans but don't love them.

For all the official statistics, by far the most visible travelers are the Japanese, and there is always at least one thirty-member Japanese group at the Duomo listening to the patter from a guide. Part of the tour includes a visit to Brunelleschi, a high-end clothing store a block from the Duomo where the Japanese happily allow themselves to be herded in as a group. Some members of the group are designer mules sent to Italy to buy well-known labels for the wealthy, with their holiday paid in return.

Yet the non-Italian language heard most on the streets is English, spoken by Americans. Either the official figures are wrong, or the Japanese are simply the most visible while the Americans are the most audible. Florentine waiters such as Antonio Belvedere praise Americans. After all, they are *his* bread and butter; he brings *their* bread and butter. The symbiotic bond works perfectly. Real estate broker Carol Milligan, who helped us find our apartment, is herself a transplanted American and firmly believes that Italians actually like Americans as a people; they just don't like American foreign policy or George W. Bush.

You don't have to search far to find the opposite view. Sandy used green plastic garden wire in a sculpture and returned to the same hardware store to buy more. When she purchased two-thirds of what remained on the spool, the sales-clerk, a man in his late thirties, commented that she must have a large garden. "Oh, no," said Sandy, "I'm a student. I'm using this for sculpture." Said he, derisively, "More Americans should come here and go to school." When she replied, "I'm not American, I'm Canadian," a smile replaced his sneer, he blew her a kiss, shouted "*Canadese*" to everyone in the store, and then launched into a rant about arrogant Americans.

Americans are their own worst enemy. They take photos with flash even when they know they shouldn't; if repri-manded they pretend they cannot comprehend even if perfect English is being spoken. They walk into a store or stride up to a museum ticket window, make no attempt at any greeting in Italian, and just assume the person they're addressing will not only understand English but will also stop whatever they're doing to serve them. If the unfortunate individual speaks no English, Americans conclude the cause can only be a hearing disorder and talk louder. At that point, someone nearby – often another customer – comes to the rescue as interpreter. The American always looks so relieved, as if civilization has somehow been saved and the United Nations functions after all.

At Beccofino, one of the finest restaurants in Florence, and one of the few with modern design and food presentation similar to the North American way of stacking food on oddly shaped plates, we watched one evening as six Americans were seated at a prime round table in the center of the room. The tray of complimentary glasses of Prosecco was on the way but had not arrived before they stormed out, miffed about some perceived slight. It couldn't have been a language issue – their waiter spoke perfect English. When we asked what happened, he said, "Some Americans are jerks." The words weren't spoken in criticism or anger; it's just how life too often is in his business.

At Pegna, an upscale grocery store near our apartment, I watched as an American man in a blue blazer barged in and began demanding truffles. When the first two staffers couldn't understand what he said, they produced an English-speaking clerk who gently informed Mr. Blazer that they weren't expecting truffles for another month. When he fell quiet at the disappointing news, the employees returned to their work.

His silence, however, did not mean he was finished demanding that the impossible be produced. Mr. Blazer soon recovered, stood in the center of the store, and loudly said, "Um." He kept repeating his monosyllabic sound, getting louder and louder as if he were a small electric motor trying to get started. When no one paid any attention – on the quite appropriate assumption that he had nothing to say – he left, shaking his head, and was probably baffled how that place he called Peg-nah had managed to stay in business since 1860.

The typical view held by most Italians came from one Italian man I won't identify, who required little to launch into an anti-American rant. "I am married to an American. I have traveled there many times," he said, thereby establishing his credentials. "But I find them very parochial. They are totally unaware of what's going on in the world yet they believe everything they have and everything they do is the best, when obviously it is not. Look at their health system! The worst part is that they believe everybody should blindly follow their lead. Iraq was a terrible mistake. We have to get our troops out of there."

No superpower will ever be popular, but arrogant Americans will continue to be resented, even reviled, until they return to a policy of isolationism, a most unlikely event. Meanwhile, I don't expect to see the president strolling down Via Roma anytime soon.

San Miniato al Monte, perched high on a hill south of Florence, is architecturally important because this church, built in the eleventh century, was one of the earliest in the city. The façade of San Miniato features green marble from Prato and white from Carrara; the combination of those colors and the rounded arches mark this style as Tuscan Romanesque.

As is the case with all Benedictine monasteries, this one was built well away from settlements. The monks like being close enough to walk into the city, buy a newspaper, and have an espresso, but they also want to be able to retreat from the hurly-burly. In the rooms where they pray the windows are placed high on the walls so they are not tempted to look outside when their minds should be focused on a higher calling.

These days, few young men are joining any of the holy orders to dedicate their lives to God so there are only ten Benedictines at San Miniato. Most of them are elderly and can be seen in their cowled white robes slipping through doorways, or sitting silently in the church with eyes closed. At 5:30 p.m., they gather in the crypt with its mismatched stone columns to sing Gregorian chants. Like the structure of the church itself, the cadences have remained unchanged for centuries.

The duties of the monks include the care and upkeep of a large cemetery. Among those buried in front of the church is Giovanni Spadolini, a prime minister of Italy who died in 1994. He was also a historian with a particular penchant for Napoleon, the little general who was born in Corsica. Spadolini's inscription couldn't be simpler:

Giovanni Spadolini
Un Italiano

Behind the church in the rest of the sacred ground ringed with rows of stately cypress and lofty pines are buried merchants, politicians, nobility – even a chef, Pellegrino Artusi, who wrote a cookbook in the nineteenth century that's still used today. There are free-standing family chapels in a variety of styles from Rococo to plain, hundreds of wall-mounted plaques, and numerous monuments that feature busts and other statuary. One particularly poignant piece of life-sized sculpture shows a young couple named Mazzone. He is proud in military uniform; she looks radiant in a summer dress. They are shown moving toward each other as if ready to embrace. He was killed in 1944 during the Second World War and she died a year later, in what agonizing pain of lost love we can never know.

Nearby, in Cappella Lorenzini, a small family chapel with a glass and wrought-iron door, is a bust with a wall plaque that announces the deceased's given name, Carlo Lorenzini, the dates of his birth and death, and the single word *Collodi*, the pen name under which in 1881 he wrote *The Adventures of Pinocchio*, one of the best-loved children's stories. Busts of other family members occupy two niches and on the floor are five baskets of flowers. But of the wooden puppet that became a real boy, there is no sign.

One hundred meters away lies Frederick Hartt who is equally famous in the world of art history. Hartt, a member of the faculty at the University of Virginia, wrote *History of Italian Renaissance Art*. The book, first published in 1970 and revised by him several times, remains the most renowned on the period.

Hartt was an elegant man who spent so much of his life in Florence that he was made an honorary citizen. David Wilkins, professor emeritus of the University of Pittsburgh, revised the book after Hartt's death in 1991 by adding more color photos and information about their patronage but he left the respected text largely unchanged. Hartt asked to be buried here under a simple flat marker with his dates, 1914–1991, his occupation, *storico dell'arte*, and his greatest honor, *cittadino onorario di Firenze*.

Cemeteries remind us that we are here but a brief time, but it was an unexpected meeting with one of the Benedictine monks that offered a compelling example of how our lives should be lived. Nicholas is slight of build and must be eighty, but his face is unlined. The small room in which we stand together is not just quiet, it was as if time has slowed down to match his measured pace. He is beyond serene; there is a stillness about him that is palpable. His head is shaved, giving added prominence to piercing eyes that seem to say, "Look within me and see what I have."

There is time for only one question. "What is it," I ask, "that you enjoy about your life?"

There is no hesitation; his response is as rhythmic as a Gregorian chant: "I am happy. I have my vocation. We live together and help each other. I live in peace and joy."

Neither better poetry nor finer philosophy have I ever heard.

I live in peace and joy.

A few days earlier we had visited the city of Lucca, an hour northwest of Florence. The prized relic in the church of San Martino is a four-meter statue of Christ on the cross, supposedly carved by Nicodemus, who, along with Joseph of Arimathea, placed Jesus in the tomb. Legend has it that the dark cedar statue arrived mysteriously in an unmanned boat on the shores of Italy during the eighth century and then was pulled overland to Lucca in a chariot by a pair of bulls. The sculpture is kept locked in a large wire cage in the middle of the church, except for September 13 when Christ is bedecked with gold jewelry – a crown, vest, shoes, and other lustrous pieces – and paraded through the streets of the city.

Skeptics, and I include myself among them when it comes to such mystical matters that must be taken on faith alone, are more likely to concur with the view that the crucified Christ was carved by someone other than Nicodemus, and done much later, perhaps in the Orient in the twelfth or thirteenth century.

But to believers, this relic – known as *Il Volto Santo* (The Holy Face) – is the actual visage of the living Christ. They firmly believe that the sculptor knew Christ when he was alive.

I'll tell you what I believe. That day, at San Miniato al Monte, I believe that through the holy face of Nicholas the Benedictine monk I was given a glimpse of God.

Florence has always attracted more than its share of eminent writers. Henry Wadsworth Longfellow, John Ruskin, Dostoevsky, and Henry James sought Florentine inspiration. Elizabeth Barrett Browning is buried in the English Cemetery. None of them, however, compare in local status with a native son, Dante Alighieri, author of *The Divine Comedy*.

Dante was not always celebrated in Florence. Early in his career, as a politician who fell from favor, he was condemned to death and then exiled. Without a home base, he drifted from city to city, finally settling in Ravenna, on the Adriatic. After Dante died of malaria in 1321 his enemies manufactured a negative image that became common wisdom. His portraits universally show him as a grumpy man in a close-fitting cloth cap with a hooked nose, protruding chin, and a face like a horse. A book on Dante, written by Jacqueline Risset, first published in France and recently translated into Italian, raises questions about this purported ugliness. She argues that he had far too many lovers during his lifetime to have looked quite so grotesque.

But of all the legends about Dante, none is more fascinating than that of the travails and travels of his bones. He was buried in the St. Francis basilica at Ravenna, two hours east of Florence, but sometime in the seventeenth century the Franciscan monks took it upon themselves to remove his bones from the sarcophagus for safekeeping. They stuffed his remains into a small fir box marked *OSSO DANTIS* (Bones of Dante) and hid the box in the brick wall of a garden outside the church. Word about the daring act and the secret location were passed down from brother to brother for the next two hundred years.

Early in the nineteenth century, the Franciscan order was repressed. The bones could have remained lost for all eternity but were discovered in 1865 and there are two versions of how that came about. The first, and most plausible, is that bricklayers found the box while repairing the wall. The second, more electrifying account, involves a local madman leading others to the location after having a vision of Dante emerging from the wall.

But how could they be certain, more than five hundred years after his death, that these really were Dante's bones? One foot was missing three toes and when they opened the sarcophagus where his remains were always thought to be, they found the missing digits. The find aroused international interest; the bones were displayed publicly in their proper anatomical position lying on white linen in a casket of glass and wrought iron and then reburied.

But Dante's perambulations were not yet over. In 1944, the local citizenry feared that Dante's bones could become German spoils of war so they were moved back to the same garden the monks had chosen, and buried this time under an ivy-covered earthen mound. There the remains lay hidden for eighteen months until the end of the war brought peace to the people, including Dante. Since 1945, the bones have been in a tomb beside the church. Or so they say.

Dante was married in Florence but he loved another, named Beatrice, who is buried in the neighborhood where they grew up together. Down the street, a nineteenth-century house is passed off to gullible tourists as his birthplace. A statue of Dante stands outside Santa Croce, a Gothic church that's home to the Franciscans, an order so popular during the Renaissance that the monks filled half the church, parishioners the other half.

Beside Dante, in front of the church steps, is a row of half a dozen street painters, their art displayed on easels. Most are men, but one among them is a woman. Bettina Raccome creates highly realistic watercolors and sells her work at prices ranging from twelve to one hundred euros. Sandy and I had first admired her paintings after we stopped to look in the window of a nearby studio and saw her working within. She looked up at us and smiled. We walked on but then decided that this was one of those Florentine encounters that kept happening to us so we went back and introduced ourselves.

The forty-five-year-old Bettina was born in Torino so has the blue eyes and blond hair of northern Italy. Her mother, a fashion stylist and graphic designer, worked from home. By the time Bettina was six, people were offering compliments on her art. "I realized I had talent. Everybody wanted my drawings." Bettina's father worked in a factory and, since such jobs were widely available, her mother convinced him to move the family to Florence because she thought it would be the best learning environment for Bettina, who was then eleven. Italian high schools are structured to serve specific aptitudes so Bettina studied only art and did not have to waste her time on subjects such as math and sciences in which she had neither interest nor talent. At eighteen she went on to the Accademia di Belle Arti (Academy of Fine Arts) that adjoins the Galleria dell'Accademia, home to Michelangelo's *David* and other inspiring works. Her professors did not try to impose any particular style. Instead, they taught drawing and painting techniques, urging students to discover and develop their own unique voice.

After graduation Bettina felt that she lacked the courage and confidence required to be an artist so she took a factory job hand-painting ceramics and papier-mâché objects. After ten years, the repetitive nature of the work eventually wore her down. "At the beginning I liked it. It was a good job. As time passed, I felt I needed to create something on my own. I could not be a factory worker."

Bettina stayed home to look after her young son and continued to paint but had no place to exhibit her work. A street artist friend encouraged her to try for one of the municipal licenses that are required to sell art to the public in Florence. She applied and not only won one of sixteen permits granted in 2000, she also was given the location that had been her first choice, Piazza Santa Croce, a few blocks from where she lives.

That first year was her most lucrative; she sold most of what she produced. Sales ran to fifteen hundred euros a month and in one hectic month hit twenty-five hundred euros. The annual fee of four hundred euros looked like a lucky lottery ticket; but after the horror of 9/11, her market collapsed. Three years later the travelers have yet to return to anything like the levels seen before the events of that terrible day. Moreover, the euro has gained strength. When the euro was introduced in 1999, it was equal to US$1.18, fell to 82 U.S. cents in 2000, reached parity in 2002, and then powered to an all-time high of US$1.37 in 2004.

As a result of the weak dollar, those American tourists who do come to Florence think twice about impulsively buying one of her paintings as a souvenir. Bettina also believes that the market has altered in another way. Buyers are more wary, even distrustful, and concerned that her paintings are reproductions, not originals. She resents having to negotiate prices and is not very good at it. "If you go to the baker, you don't quibble. Why quibble with the artist? But all the guide books tell them to."

From April through November Bettina spends four days a week, five hours at a stretch, in front of Santa Croce. The rest of the week she paints in her street-level studio. In the colder months, from December through March, there are no sales at all. Bettina's annual income is so low she doesn't even bother to add it up so has no idea what it is. Fortunately the Italian tax collector doesn't care about artists and artisans who make meager amounts. "It would be crucifying if you sold everything by books and receipts. A certain part of your earnings has to be taken on the sly. The authorities know; everybody does it." Her husband teaches school so they have sufficient family income for themselves and their son, now eleven, without worrying about her contribution.

Despite the difficulties, Bettina loves her work. "It doesn't sound noble, but it is a good job. I meet people. I don't have my head in a sketchbook." She paints what buyers want – scenes of Florence. "Everybody does Ponte Vecchio but everybody does it in their own way. When someone sees a painting – and likes it – that's genuine." Most buyers also want a photo of themselves with the artist and she cheerfully complies. "It makes me happy. It's a personal success. That feedback makes you want to work."

Some watercolor artists are all slap-dash and can mass-produce finished works in a few minutes even while they sit on the street. Bettina is a perfectionist who works slowly, painting only in her studio, because that's where she can achieve the high realism she wants. Sometimes a painting changes along the way, becoming different from what she originally had in mind, a transformation that would be impossible amid the dis-tractions of tourist traffic. "I enjoy art. I know I am good at it. Being an artist is a need. It is like a lifeline." She recently saw an

exhibit by Pedro Cano, a Spanish watercolor artist, who was offering his florals for sale at fifteen thousand euros. "He was very good, but he was missing a little soul. When I am his age, I will cost more. I have a lot to learn, but I'll get there."

Meanwhile, she has family responsibilities and cannot spend the sustained time she knows she needs in order to become as good as she is convinced she one day will be. "When I work, I could go on and on. I don't recognize time. I need that freedom." For now, she has to break that concentration and put down her brush when her son comes home from school or family mealtime arrives. "Although watercolor has a history of being done quickly, I feel it can become a form of art that can be very profound." She aspires to create such art, show her work in galleries, and charge Pedro Cano prices. This afternoon, however, Piazza Santa Croce beckons. Someone will have an irresistible impulse to buy the perfect Ponte Vecchio or a delightful Duomo to take home as a souvenir and Bettina Raccone has just the work to fulfill his or her whim.

❈

Ravenna, guardian of Dante's bones, is also home to some of the finest Byzantine mosaics in the land. With its lustrous golden-hued buildings, Ravenna is a very different city than stern-stoned Florence. It was here that the early image makers tried out various versions of how Christ would look and act. One rendition of *The Last Supper* shows Christ and his disciples reclining in the Roman style rather than sitting at a long table. In the fifth-century mausoleum of Galla Placidia, Christ appears as a clean-shaven young Adonis with blond hair and blue eyes, sitting among lambs. In the nearby church of San Vitale, he is similarly blond, and shown perched on a sphere of blue lapis lazuli, the most expensive color of its day. In the arch of that same church, however, the image makers have moved on to what became the accepted view. They decided that the Christ who would preside on Judgment Day should look more serious so He was given dark hair, a flowing beard, and watchful eyes.

The architects also tried to help humanity achieve harmony with God. San Vitale, erected in the sixth century, is an octagon that can be inscribed into a circle so you can stand at one point, be equidistant from all the outside walls, and feel in mystical union with God and His universe. When the best-known architect of the Renaissance, Filippo Brunelleschi, began designing churches in the fifteenth century he sought to create similarly harmonious spaces. In the Florentine churches of Santo Spirito and San Lorenzo, for example, the domes are half a hemisphere which, if completed downward into a full circle, would have their lower edge precisely halfway to the floor. A gray line on the floor is not just a geometric pattern; it divides the church in two and tells you how to read what the architect wrote. The outer aisles beyond the row of columns on either side are half the width of the central area. The square created where the transepts and main church meet is a specific size that is repeated throughout the church. All such elements are meant to satisfy the eye, soothe the soul, and create tranquility.

Once you are aware of Brunelleschi's proportional

planning, it is an obvious method to achieve a pleasing effect. But even when you are unaware of what he did or how he did it, you can still have a mystical experience with the vital force of God. Mind you, as the years passed, other architects ruined much of his work by adding ornamented altars and rebuilding interiors to hold more worshippers, thereby jarring the agreeable balance. Domes that he would have preferred be left bare became cluttered with frescoes to fool the eye with their puttis and saints and skies, a phoniness Brunelleschi detested.

What happened to Brunelleschi continues to occur. Our lives start out simply enough, and then they become stressed. In the six months prior to our departure for Florence, my blood pressure – which had for years been a rock-solid and respectable 137/78 – skyrocketed to 190/90 and remained stuck there. Anxiety about the life change we were contemplating was the obvious cause but the pounding headaches and tingling in my feet and hands finally caused Sandy to take me one August Saturday evening to Toronto General Hospital. They conducted tests, assured me I had not suffered a stroke, and sent me home.

Our time here has healed me, as if I have come under the protection of Nicolai Stenonis, the only saint who is buried in Florence. You don't have to pay an admission to pay your respects and ask for his help, just slip in the side door of San Lorenzo and tell the attendant your mission is to visit his tomb that's littered with beseeching missives – long letters on fine vellum about personal problems, Post-it Notes asking for his intervention with some matter – so many paper pleas that from time to time church officials have to sweep the stone clean and collect all the notes. He will not grant requests for financial favors but many are the stories about how supplicants at the tomb of Stenonis – or their suffering loved ones – have been helped through their faith in him. Scoffers beware; something's happening here.

❧

As religious as Italy is, with priests and nuns a part of everyday street life, Italian television presents the profane. In my quest to improve my language skills, I decide to watch some television daily in the hopes of picking up new phrases and the correct pronunciation.

There's plenty of choice. Among the fifty channels we receive, only MTV is in English. Two channels are in Arabic and the rest are in Italian and include the usual news, soccer games, and bicycle races that never seem to reach the finish line. There are also familiar home shopping formats: carpets at 40 per cent off, bun-burning machines for four easy payments, bespangled brooches, and youth-restoring face creams. Entertainment channels show movies that have been dubbed in Italian: *Dances with Wolves* and *Return of the Pink Panther*. There are syndicated American TV shows such as *Columbo* and *Walker, Texas Ranger*, or you can watch Calista Flockhart fall in and out of love all over again in *Ally McBeal*. There's even a channel offering the same Popeye cartoons I watched as a boy in the 1950s. Once upon a time, Italian directors such as Federico Fellini and Michelangelo Antonioni told great stories in film. Now, Italians seem good only at dubbing. Like Canada, useful for Hollywood production because of tax breaks, both countries seem to have become the running dogs of U.S. cultural imperialism.

The main reason Italian television seems to exist is to feed that most popular of all Italian male pastimes, watching beautiful women. There are two fashion channels with endless parades of runway models in bikinis and sheer clothing. Sunscreen ads show topless women on a beach. Italy's version of *Who Wants to Be a Millionaire?* features women in the front row of the audience wearing halter-tops and short shorts, no matter the season. There's a beauty-contest channel conducting a never-ending search among the teenagers of Tuscany. It's a wonder there are any women left on the streets of Florence – by now they should all be in a TV studio somewhere.

Even the nightly sportscast on Rete 37 is not exempt. Four men in suits and ties sit behind individual desks and talk animatedly about the day's events and tomorrow's contests. In the middle of the foursome is a young woman perched on a high stool. Unlike her male confreres, she has been provided with no modesty panel, the better for the viewer to admire her legs rising to a skirt so short it barely covers her navel. She holds a sheaf of papers, as if she is supposed to have a role, but is never called upon to comment. Surprisingly, the four men don't so much as sneak a peek at her, so keen are they to argue about Juventus or AC Milan. Only the cameraman pays attention. Every few seconds, while the men gab, there's a full shot showing off her shapely legs or a closeup that captures her cleavage. No words, only a world-weary smile, escape her lips.

When Rete 37 broadcasts a soccer game, the commentators

sit in stadium booths that are exposed to the elements. On cool days the men wear warm coats and hats but the requisite distracting damsel wears a silk blouse with a plunging neckline. Again the camera lovingly caresses her chest, her face, or her legs every few seconds.

This sexist view of women has seeped into many institutions. Porn star Ilona Staller, known as *Cicciolina* (Cuddles), was elected to Parliament and served for five years. Italian pro golfer Sophie Sandolo sells a calendar with a provocative cover shot that shows her lying on her back, topless, with hips rampant. "Italy," writes author Tobias Jones in *The Dark Heart of Italy*, "is the land that feminism forgot."

Striscia la Notizia, a nightly TV show, has both a male and female presenter with their names displayed on their shared desk – E. Greggio and M. Hunziker. Somehow I can't imagine Jay Leno with a nameplate. Ezio Greggio launches the show with some warm-up banter to get the studio audience in the mood for the fun to follow. His act includes video clips of bloopers from other networks such as a crowded finale on stage where one of the show's participants mistakenly whacks another in the nose as they all wave good-bye.

Greggio's monologue is mere prelude for the arrival of his co-host, Michelle Hunziker, a Swiss-born supermodel. She is beautiful, blond, has a relentless smile with impossibly perfect teeth, and always wears outfits with plunging décolletage. She doesn't walk onto the set or appear through a parted curtain, she dances across the stage, twirling her skirt, showing off her thighs, and laughing all the way. Between segments, two women dressed like cheerleaders for the Dallas Cowgirls do a dance-pole number more appropriate for a strip bar. When the routine is over, they kneel on the desk on each side of the hosts, like leggy lionesses guarding the gate. They are *velina*, an interesting Italian word that has gone through a series of iterations. At one time, *velina* was the carbon paper used for typewritten copies. In politics, it's a government order to impose, say, media censorship. Now, it's the eye candy that helps move a show along.

Mai Dire is a combination interview and game show littered with beautiful women who line up half a dozen at a time in scanty outfits to jiggle and giggle with the hosts. The male host is a head shorter than his female counterpart and nowhere near as handsome as she is pretty. Presumably such a mismatch is purposeful so that male viewers can feel superior and say, "Well, I'm taller than him and certainly better looking. I could get that job and be with those women if only I could catch a break."

The show also features a studio audience that applauds on cue but the only members of the public who get any face time on camera are – you guessed it – pretty women who have been planted like birds of paradise in an otherwise bleak garden. The job of the two hosts is to talk loudly and lure women onto the set. If the producer feels the pace is lagging, someone truly ridiculous will appear, maybe a man dressed like a squirrel. When that segment has mercifully finished, it's back to what passes for normal. That could mean sending the girls to clamber along a slippery arch that rises high above the stage. The contest seems to involve how fast they can travel wearing heels, measured in meters per minute, and how far up their skirts we can see, measured in millimeters, there not being that much material to matter.

At least *Mai Dire* has a sense of humor. One night, three men pretend to be the Bee Gees in a taped segment. They wear flowing wigs, sing in falsetto voices, and are dressed in white suits to mimic John Travolta in *Saturday Night Fever*. The three paparazzi track down some politicians who awkwardly participate in an impromptu song-and-dance routine. They also discover Tom Hanks, but he is leaving his hotel so the actor only has time for a few awkward arm movements in sync with their singing before speeding away.

Then the trio comes upon the sultan of strut, John Travolta himself, at the Westin Excelsior. He smiles affably but really doesn't want to be any part of their skit. They convince him to shuffle a few dance steps, but he wisely declines to wear either the proffered white jacket or the black wig. When they make their final plea, telling him their dream has been "to strut with John Travolta" he reluctantly yields and soon it was as if they were all on the pavements of New York, heading for a night on the town. Strutting.

But strutting, I have concluded, was not invented by John Travolta in that 1977 film, nor did writer Tom Wolfe identify its beginnings in the 1960s when he wrote about the "pimp roll" of certain young black men on the prowl. Strutting combusted long ago on the streets of Italy. This week I saw two young men with chiseled good looks strutting in such a manner that even I stopped in my tracks to watch. They wore black suits, black t-shirts, and glinting gold neck chains as they walked lightly on the balls of their feet in a measured pace with heads held high, elbows cocked, shoulders and hips swinging in syncopation but in opposite directions. A clutch of female American tourists also stopped to stare, their mouths actually hanging open at the macho sight of such raw testosterone. Shouted one of the ladies, "You're looking good, honey." Without breaking stride, one of the men rotated his torso toward her, smiled, turned away, and carried on, already convinced of the truth of her statement.

In Italy, if you're a man, all you have to do is look good. In Lucca, the tomb of Ilaria del Carretto, one of the most beautiful sculptures in the land, features a dog at her feet, a symbol of Ilaria's loyalty to her husband. Safe to say, there are no monuments to Italian males accompanied by their devoted dogs. One survey found that 75 per cent of Italian men admitted to having an affair, although part of the explanation for such a high proportion was that some respondents felt it was the expected answer so they'd better give it.

Like those two strutting studs of today, for centuries the men of Florence have drawn attention to themselves through their dress and deportment. An exhibit in the Pitti Palace sponsored by Pucci included his couturier designs from the 1970s as well as some garments worn by the Medicis, the bankers and art patrons who ran Renaissance Florence.

The bodies of Cosimo I, his wife Eleonara, and their seventh son, Don Garzia, were recently exhumed. After their clothing was carefully restored, the experts concluded they had been buried in everyday wear, not ceremonial attire, because Don Garzia's doublet had an elbow patch typical of an active young man. As his parents' favorite child, he had been put in charge of the Tuscan navy at thirteen and the pope made him an honorary commander of the papal fleet.

Don Garzia was only fifteen when he died of malaria in 1562. To me, the most interesting aspect of this powerful young man's carefully preserved outfit was the codpiece. This was not just the cup-shaped pouch of cloth covering the groin of some aging male courtier in Elizabethan England. No, the Florentine version was an upward projection large enough to hold an erect penis and then some. As if the size, position, and compass direction of the thrusting crotch weren't sufficient to dazzle a passerby, the cloth of the codpiece was ribbed and decorated. The entire contraption was hinged with a knotted cord that, when undone, could unleash that which lay within for a call of nature or some other more amorous cause. As Don Garzia strutted past, his codpiece at rigid salute, the women of that era likely thought of him using similarly salivating words to those "looking good" ladies of today.

It is 9 a.m. on a Saturday morning and another sort of Renaissance procession is moving its way slowly through central Florence. The gait is measured, the costumes a riot of color, and the music appropriately ornate. Leading the way are helmeted men bearing pikes, followed by drummers and trumpeters, more pike carriers, and then women in velvet gowns with puffy sleeves, pearl necklaces, and pearl earrings. From time to time, three men fire a round from a small cannon on wheels they are hauling along.

All the men wear pantaloons and doublets in various combinations of red and white, yellow and blue, or red and blue. They have breastplates of either metal or leather, and their wide-brimmed hats sprout long feathered plumes in red, yellow, and blue. I look to see if anyone in costume is suppressing a grin, fearful they might look foolish, but no one is cracking a smile. Time travel is not to be taken lightly. I can hardly wait to find an empty stretch of street to see if I can copy their measured gait, with one foot slowly moving in front of the other and then allowed to hang in the air, just for a second, before being placed carefully on the cobblestones.

The reason for the pageant this morning is the 150th anniversary of the founding of the municipal police. It's too early for tourists in the Piazza del Duomo, so the onlookers are by far outnumbered by scores of police on foot, on horseback, and on motorcycle, their tall white helmets shining in the sun. The costumed marchers arrange themselves in ranks awaiting the dignitaries while organizers mill about nervously at the door of the nearby Baptistery. First to arrive for the ceremony are some uniformed military, followed by city officials in suits, a priest, and then two nuns who scuttle by almost as an afterthought, a small scrim of unnecessary punctuation in an otherwise important sentence.

Trumpets announce the police honor guard, men and women marching in rows of three, carefully arranged by height, shortest at the front. The costumed medieval participants place right foot behind bent left leg and make a graceful sweeping bow with hat in hand as the police leadership marches by, each man wearing more braid and badges than the last, until finally the golden-shouldered chief takes the salute before stepping past the bronze door reliefs and into the Baptistery.

Such a pageant, such colors. It could just as well be 1460. The next to appear might be Cosimo de Medici himself on his massive steed. Cosimo is not well, as everyone knows, so there is much speculation about when his son, Piero, will succeed him. But Piero has the gout and isn't expected to last. Those in the know say that the better ruler will eventually be the grandson, Lorenzo the Magnificent, who has wisely decided to be elsewhere this morning rather than play third fiddle. The man may have no sense of smell but he knows when to stay away. Something about having business in Rome.

NOVEMBER

WE TOOK SOME ITALIAN LESSONS before we left Toronto, but there was too much happening in those final weeks, little time for homework, and so our progress was limited. My vocabulary has grown substantially, but lengthy conversation is still not easy.

Classes in *Italiano per stranieri* (Italian for foreigners) are held near Santa Croce in a 1960s building that's slightly decrepit and rife with graffiti. A dozen of us gather at 3:30 p.m. and sit two per table in Room 27 on the fourth floor, the preserve of Senora Alberti, a peppery woman with frizzy black hair. Senora Alberti is so short that when she walks past the seated students, she looks directly in your eyes, a very effective teaching technique. My seatmate is Ingrid from Sweden. On her left is Raoul from Iran. Ingrid speaks some English, Raoul none. He speaks French, she does not. They converse in Persian. She introduces him to me by explaining that his wife is married to her husband. I let it pass. In language class, one must be forgiving.

In keeping with the changing flow of local immigration, in the second row sit four Chinese students with a Chinese woman who appears to be their minder. To my right are four Spaniards, a young woman with flashing eyes and three young men who look like soccer players. We spend the first twenty minutes filling out forms. Passports are taken away, photocopied, and returned. I think that now makes fourteen separate agencies of the Italian government that possess my personal details.

The room we're in must have previously been used for anatomy classes. On the walls are half a dozen framed drawings showing specific muscle groups such as the arm, the leg, the throat. There is also a black-and-white drawing of some he-man in an impossible pose with his fists clenched above his head, his powerful legs bent at the knees, every muscle a-ripple. In the right-front corner, perched on a high table and propped on a stick, is a skeleton with no skull and no feet, a reminder of what can happen to language school dummies.

At first, there is a gentle pace and an air of polite formality to the proceedings. *"Come si chiama?"* Even a two-year-old knows his name but I'm proud to have cleared the first hurdle. The next round of questions, posed first to the Spaniards, involve how many brothers and sisters they have. As an only child, I'm ready with my answer, but when Senora Alberti points her stubby finger in my face I get a complicated inquiry about my grandparents. I fall into stunned silence. She clucks her tongue and, with air of sadness, moves on. Ingrid has a sister, Raoul two brothers. I was the only one asked about forebears who are dead and gone. The skeleton rattles a femur.

The Spaniards, it soon becomes apparent, are fluent in Italian. They chat easily with the teacher, laugh heartily at each other's jokes, and discuss dancing at the disco where they drank too much Jägermeister. They regard the rest of us as if we are bodies that have recently washed up on shore. In the row behind, the Chinese students are still struggling to fill out their forms. They will neither speak nor be spoken to during the ninety-minute class.

Soon I am equally lost amid a flurry of definitive articles and a fog of prepositions. I begin to see the skeleton as a symbol of my predicament: no head for languages and no feet with which to catch up. I hear the word *fratelli* and snap to attention. Maybe this is another chance to talk about my lack of brothers and make my grandparents proud, but the moment passes.

Finally there's another word I recognize, *finito*. It's 5 p.m., quitting time. Before I can escape, Senora Alberti plunks down the textbook I must buy if I am to continue. The cover features that fearsome word *grammar* but I press on, asking "*Quanto costa?*" She turns the book over to show the price – 36.15 euros, almost C$60. "*Domani?*" she wonders. I shake my head no – I will not be coming tomorrow. I could not have hurt her more had she been the Virgin Mary pierced by the seven swords representing the seven sorrows. Hands splayed and fluttering on her bosom, she staggers backward, then surges toward me, demanding to know what I do for a living. "*Scrittore Canadese,*" I reply. The sunshine of a bright idea lights up her face. She tells me to remain seated, rushes out of the room, and returns a few minutes later to say that I'm to arrive early tomorrow at which time I will be introduced to an Italian writer. The purpose of the meeting is not clear but she hints that he will help me unlock the language of Dante, we being kindred spirits and all.

The other students have long since left. Out of the corner of my eye I see three clementine oranges under the chair where the Spanish woman sat. I promise I'll show up tomorrow. I am curious to meet this writer. Failing that, I wonder if I could learn how to lay McIntosh apples under my chair like some chicken in a henhouse.

Signora Alberti greets me the next afternoon like a lost lamb that strayed from the fold. She scurries away and returns with a cheerful, balding man of fifty named Mori Siro. It crosses my mind that Mori Siro must either be a pen name or one of those riddling anagrams. In the brief time during which that thought came and went, it became clear that this encounter has nothing at all to do with helping me. Did I know a translator and a publisher in Canada who could help distribute his detective novels? I did not, but agreed to take his name and address, assuring him I'd be in touch if any such information came to hand. Our conversation over, I notice that other students are arriving for class. This time, I find my feet, and I flee. For good. My trusty Collins phrase book has begun to look pretty appealing. It makes no demands and has the pleasing attribute of already being purchased. As Mori Siro himself might say, *habeas corpus*. Without my body in that anatomy room, no one can turn me into the victim that is so essential in every murder mystery.

❧

Initially, I knew about twenty words in Italian and six of them were *prego*, a multipurpose word with many meanings. The most common use is when a person says *grazie*, "thank you," and you say *prego*, for "you're welcome" or "not at all." If you open a door and indicate to a woman she should precede you, you say *prego*. When you enter a restaurant, a waiter may say *prego*, as in "come in" or "at your service," or he'll say *prego* when he delivers dinner, as in "there you go." In a store, if there are several people waiting, the clerk will say *prego* for "who's next?" If you didn't hear something, you can ask, "*Prego*?" as in "Excuse me?"

Over time my vocabulary grew and my language skills improved, but not to the point where I ever was able to talk easily in Italian. It's hard learning a new language at sixty. Unlike in French, where so many English words have been embraced that official committees have been created to fret about the purity of the language, there are very few anglicized words in Italian. Once while I was on an elevator with three other people, a man attempted to board until someone said "*jam paco*" and closed the door in his face, but other than that I heard few such adopted phrases.

My French is much better than my Italian, but then again I've been at it longer. I studied French in high school and worked in Ottawa for five years where I took a Berlitz immersion course. I got to the point where I could understand most speeches given in French in Parliament. We rented the same house for summer holidays most years during the 1990s in a tiny village in France where I could make myself understood in a place where no English is spoken. My French vocabulary is sizable but, even after all those years of regular use, I would never call myself bilingual.

As a result, I knew that real progress during our time in Florence would be unlikely. Some lessons come early. The *C* on the taps does not mean cold, it stands for *calda*, hot. Cold is *freddo*, how you want your white wine. I eventually came to speak what I call "fruit and vegetable" Italian. As part of my contribution to running the household, I did most of the food shopping, so I soon learned the words of many food items as well as descriptives for slice and volume and type. Even so, I was able to buy a lot of items simply by pointing and saying "*questo*," which means "this." Less commonplace products can be more problematic. I needed to clear a slow drain in our flat, but my fumbling phrases were getting me nowhere at the hardware store where I had previously been able to ask for light bulbs, garbage bags, and glue. Finally, I pulled out a piece of paper and drew a sink, complete with an S-shape pipe and a clog. "*Disgorgione*" declared the clerk, a word so perfect for the product it was a wonder I hadn't guessed on my own the noun I needed.

Every other week I walk east for fifteen minutes with my bundle buggy to Standa, the nearest large grocery store, to load up on bulky items like paper products and six-packs of two-liter bottled water. En route I always take a deep breath and try and look innocent as I pass the main branch of the Banca d'Italia. The sidewalk is narrow and there is no margin for error as I sidle by the uniformed officer carrying a machine gun on a shoulder sling, with his trigger finger at the ready. What if a wheel of my cart falls off, as it usually does sometime during the outing, sending tomatoes in all directions? Will he shoot first and inspect my goods later?

Lucca, the Standa butcher, insists on speaking English to me; I am equally persistent in speaking Italian to him. When I ask for 150 grams of *prosciutto cotto*, he always repeats my order in English: "fresh ham." If I ask for *pollo* he will say "chicken," pronouncing each syllable separately as if he's teaching me my own mother tongue. I can use all the help I can get. At one restaurant, I carefully choose two courses, both of which turn out to be risotto, the only Italian dish I don't like. How stupid is that? The first time I tried to order some fancy drinks I asked for *due mimosa bellini*, then sat back to bask in my sophistication. "No," said the waiter politely, "you can have mimosa *or* bellini, but you can't have both." Each is a pleasant and potent concoction made with Prosecco, a sparkling wine, but mimosa is made with orange juice, bellini uses peach. Now I know the difference, a learning experience I'm happy to repeat whenever the constituent parts are available.

Sandy speaks less Italian than I do, but that doesn't stop her from communicating easily with people who speak no English – she uses a combination of body language and the sheer exuberance of her personality. At the Thursday flower market, a compliment about a vendor's necklace precipitates a lesson about extending the life of tulips. The vendor removes her earring and then uses it to pierce the stem of the tulip just below the bloom, a tip her grandmother taught her that makes tulips sit up straight in the vase.

While I enjoyed food shopping at the two-storey Mercato Centrale, for my daily rounds I preferred a row of stores five minutes away from our flat on Via dei Cerchi, which I called Alimentary Alley, with two butchers, a fishmonger, and two fruit and vegetable stands. Everyone is happy to see me and they sell top-quality goods. Here they speak only Italian and help me learn a few words every time I shop. *Prosciutto cotto* is correctly pronounced **cawww**-toe, by drawing out the first syllable. If you cut it off short, and say both syllables quickly with equal stress, no one understands what you want because there are at least half a dozen varieties of *prosciutto* available.

Around the corner on Via dei Tavolini is Cantinetta dei Verrazzano where they have the best bread in the city, plus slices of fresh focaccia topped with a wide range of herbs, cheeses, tomatoes, zucchini flowers, and prosciutto for a tasty lunch. Verrazzano also boasts Alberto, a cheerful barista who serves excellent coffee. Gilli is equally good, but mostly because of the wood-and-glass surroundings as well as the view, which looks out onto the lively expanse of Piazza della Repubblica.

Like Lucca of Standa, all vendors have their own quirks. For example, each seems to have a different way of asking, "Do you want anything else?" At the fruit and vegetable stand, they say "*Dopo?*" while they pick out your four artichokes. *Dopo* does not refer to my intelligence, it means "after" or "next?" At Pegna, as they carve your piece of cheese from the wheel of Gorgonzola, they say something that sounds like "*oi*" which is definitely the least gracious of all the possibilities. At Verrazzano, it's the more pleasant "*Basta cosi?*" which literally means "Is that enough?" but has the sense of "Is that everything?"

Italians instinctively know how much is enough. There are no obese Italians; there is no wretched excess, only joy in everyday pursuits. I stood one evening in our favorite neighborhood pizzeria, Antica Nuti, waiting for my takeout *quattro stagione* to be pulled on a paddle from the wood-fired oven and watched in amazement as one of the waiters delivered dinner to a patron while dancing down the aisle in time to the music on the speaker system. When next he passed, I said, "I've heard of singing waiters, but I've never seen a dancing waiter." "I love my job," he replied, and whirled away even more joyously.

The rains in Venice began at 4 a.m. on a Sunday morning. Six hours later, opening time at the Peggy Guggenheim Collection, the contemporary art museum on the Grand Canal, and everyone was up to the gunwales in water. The rain has stopped but so much fell in such a short time that the result is what's called *acqua alta*, high water, when a combination of rain and rising tide seeps up through the stone pavement, slurps over the canal walls, and floods the streets. On this day the water is almost knee-deep. The scene is surreal, but by *acqua alta* standards this is nothing. Residents wear rubber boots and blithely go about their daily business. Unequipped visitors remove shoes and socks, roll up pant legs, hike skirts, and generally make do. Being in line for ten minutes awaiting the museum opening leaves high-water marks on pantyhose and bare legs alike, not to mention a certain blue tinge to the skin, given the chilly temperature of the sea water in November. The only individual who is safely dry is the equestrian rider in the courtyard by twentieth-century Italian sculptor Marino Marini. The male figure on the horse leans back in an exultant pose, arms spread, an erect penis pointing Heavenward like a lightning rod looking for a jolt.

Acqua alta is a perennial problem in Venice. The city is built on more than two hundred islands, all at sea level. On any given day, Piazza San Marco, the main square, will have small pools of water in various places. Trestles topped with flat boards are always at the ready, stacked against the walls. If the water rises, the trestles are quickly put in place for tourists to stand on, high and dry, as they line up to enter the cathedral.

We'd previously eaten at a café that had three rows of tables at the edge of the Grand Canal with views of the Rialto. As the evening passes and water begins lapping at our feet, the waiter tells us to rest our shoes on the table legs. As the water rises higher, the waiters put on rubber boots and shuffle everyone to slightly higher ground closer to the wall. A Japanese man is so delighted with what's happening that he refuses to move. His unhappy wife, who is not as enamored with the rising tide, takes off her shoes and puts her feet on his lap under the table.

A siren sounds in the distance. A waiter shouts, "Ambulance coming, raise your feet." Obediently we do so and, sure enough, as the ambulance boat passes, the wake rolls by underneath us. Without the warning we would have been wet to the knees. By now, the Japanese man is gleefully crouching on the seat of his chair, motioning to his wife to do the same. She refuses, her face close to her dinner plate in embarrassment, her legs propped on his chair. The waiters scrunch our tables closer to the wall, where the water is somewhat shallower.

Another siren wails in the distance, "Ambulance coming, ambulance coming," shouts the Japanese man, laughing all the while. Finally, the water is too high for continued dining and we're told to move inside. The waiters line up rows of chairs so the marooned can bump their way to the door of the restaurant by hiking themselves on their bums, legs raised, from one chair seat to the next. The Japanese gentleman reluctantly agrees, but, game to the end, as he hoists himself to safety he calls, "Last man out."

In the night, there's more rain accompanied by lightning. We move our suitcases onto the spare bed to keep our clothing dry in the unlikely event that *acqua alta* reaches us two floors above the canal in our rental apartment. In the morning, we are dry, but so certain am I that *acqua alta* will have filled every alley and covered all the piazzas that I convince Sandy we should wear borrowed boots and raincoats. At the last minute, I stick rainhats into the pockets, just in case.

During the ten-minute walk to Piazza San Marco, we see no one else dressed for Noah's flood. Fools, I think, where's their good sense? At San Marco, the sun is shining, the pavement is bone dry. People gather round, eyeing us like we might be prophets, newly arrived from some mountaintop, with an important announcement about pending disaster. In desperation, I shout, "Ambulance coming, ambulance coming." Amid the ensuing melee, we escape, strip off our raingear, and hike back to the apartment with everything balled up under our arms. I hear a noise. Is it the bubble of *acqua alta* at my feet? Will I be redeemed? No, it's that throaty noise that women make when they are exasperated with their men.

❖

After two months of admiring Brunelleschi's Dome from various angles, it's time for a climb on this mild, sunny, and windless November day. Unlike tourist season, when there might be dozens on line, today there is no one. Entrance to the Duomo is free, but walking to the top costs six euros. The first 50 steps up the narrow, spiraling staircase pass by quickly, but by the time I reach a stopping point after 150 steps, I'm about ready for a breather. There's a display of various mechanical instruments and tools that were used to erect the dome or cupola. After fifty years of deliberation about the roofless cathedral, work began in 1420 and was finally finished in 1436. The display of scaffolding, buckets, trestles, winches, and pulleys gives some idea of the enormity of building a dome on a base that began 170 meters up in the air. The massive result, rising a further 40 meters, is bigger than either St. Paul's in London or the Capitol in Washington, D.C.

About halfway, after 250 steps, I've reached the interior balcony at the base of the dome. As I look up at the massive fresco on the dome's interior, I know that architect Filippo Brunelleschi would not have approved of this later addition. Still, *The Last Judgement* by Giorgio Vasari is magnificent.

There's a cherub peeking out from under the robe of the enthroned Christ as those who have been saved gather round. Even the fallen Adam and Eve are now forgiven and in His presence. On the other side of the dome, as far removed from Christ as possible, are the devils and the damned. Leering beasts and seven-headed serpents chew at sinners and spit out skeletons while other sorry reprobates are pitch-forked into the abyss. Perhaps those tossed down get a second chance to climb back, like a life-and-death game of snakes and ladders.

As I work my way higher on the same sandstone steps used by the laborers who built the dome, the space grows narrow and claustrophobic. I'm actually climbing between the dome's two concentric shells. The inner one, the thicker of the two, is two meters wide at the base and one and a half meters wide at the top. The outer shell is much narrower, only sixty centimeters at the bottom and half that at the top. Despite the copious amount of research conducted by Ross King, author of the best-selling *Brunelleschi's Dome*, the full scope of the architect's methods remain a mystery more than five centuries later. Here and there a row of bricks appears, including the odd bit in a herringbone pattern, as well as hints of the beams and iron chains that helped hold the cantilevered structure in place as masons worked their way skyward without benefit of centering devices or wooden scaffolding.

Every so often along the way, a porthole in the outer wall offers views of the city's tile roofs, a church, or the far-off Tuscan hillside. While the openings serve as modern-day lookouts, they had a structural function as well so the wind could whistle through, thereby reducing the force exerted on the dome. Over the years many of Brunelleschi's seventy-two original vents have been closed for various reasons and that may be a contributing cause of the dome's deterioration. The rumble of modern-day traffic at the base didn't help either, so most of the surrounding area was turned into a pedestrian-only zone some twenty-five years ago.

The last 40 steps are the worst. They rise at a steep angle that feels like sixty degrees. The ceiling is low; I have to duck. There are iron railings on either side of the stairs with which to haul yourself up, but no Sherpas to help in this final push to the summit. All is quiet except for the sound of your own quickened heartbeat and panting breath reverberating off the walls.

Daylight at last! After thirty minutes and 463 steps, I've reached the viewing platform that encircles the top of the dome. At eleven in the morning, there are but ten other hardy souls up here. The views are astounding, perhaps as far as twenty kilometers to snow-capped peaks on the northern horizon. Tourists below are mere specks on the pavement. Florentine landmarks are readily identifiable. Just naming those covered in scaffolding for restoration yields a lengthy list: Santa Croce, the Uffizi Gallery, Palazzo Vecchio, Santo Spirito, and the Synagogue.

I am a hundred meters from the ground, the equivalent height of a thirty-storey building, and the marble lantern above me rises a further thirty-five meters. This is the octagonal structure under restoration that I asked Signor Bianchi about on that first day we arrived. For all the scaffolding that encases the lantern with its tall windows to let light into the cathedral, there's not a worker in sight. *Infinito* indeed.

The marble platform on which I'm standing slopes toward the edge so that rain can run into the gutter. Around the edge there's a waist-high mesh fence and an iron railing. The angle not only accentuates the height but the minimal fencing also gives you the sense that one misstep would hurl you downward like the damned in Vasari's fresco.

And there below, at a forty-five-degree angle past Giotto's Campanile, is Via Roma 3. Just as the Londoner born within earshot of Bow Bells can call himself a Cockney, I can now say, *Io sono fiorentino di Cupolone.* I am a Florentine from the great dome. Our apartment windows are easily identifiable, third and fourth from the corner. Until last week, four clay pots of pink cyclamen sat on one of our window ledges. A hundred-kilometer wind came howling through one night and blew off two of the pots. They tumbled to the pavement five floors below and were smashed to bits. We rescued the other two plants at 4 a.m. and they now bloom happily inside. In real life, as in frescoes, there are the saved and there are the damned.

Tamp, tamp, tamp. Ron Cook is packing coffee grounds to produce cups of espresso on a very special machine in the reception area of his company, La Marzocco. This four-spigot appliance, finished with hand-hammered brass, was made by Bruno Bambi who, along with his brother, Giuseppe, founded the firm in 1927. Piero, son of Giuseppe, still comes to work daily and is in his eighties. Cook, president and a part owner with other investors who bought La Marzocco from the family, has not only treasured the company traditions but also modernized its business methods.

But first, the coffee. Tamp, tamp, tamp, into the handled holder that's clamped onto the machine. The water is heated to 93°C in a stainless steel boiler, the heart of the internal mechanics, and then takes about twenty seconds to flow through the coffee into the waiting cup below.

Espresso is more than just a flavorful drink – it's an integral part of daily life in Italy. There's a bar on every block, where men and women of all ages stand and drink their espressos several times a day. There is a sense of occasion to the proceedings that's about as far from a Tim Hortons double double as you can possibly get. These cups are porcelain, the countertop is marble, and the serving staff are often jacketed. The surroundings range from frescoes and chandeliers for the hoity-toity to tile and wood for the hoi-polloi.

Whether the patron is moneyed or middle-class, espresso offers a quick pick-me-up, a time for some social discourse, a stop before mass. To be sure, the moment can be fleeting. The small amount of hot liquid is downed quickly, in three successive sips with the cup poised in mid-air, not placed on the saucer, between swallows. A cream-filled *bombolone* in the other hand can disappear just as speedily.

Despite the pace, niceties are observed. The patrons and the baristas always exchange greetings at the time the order is placed. When the patron leaves, there's a round of good-byes as well. An espresso may cost only eighty-five cents, but there's an appropriate way of doing things, a procedure unchanged for decades, even in the most modest of establishments.

Such haunts and habits are Ron Cook's market. La Marzocco makes espresso machines in the village of Pian di San Bartolo twelve kilometers north of Florence. Born in Rochester, New York, Cook and his wife, Jean, lived briefly in Milan in the 1990s, returned to the United States, and then were wooed back to Italy in 1995 by a group of U.S. and foreign investors who bought La Marzocco. Cook's professional background includes food sales and management. He helped build a pasta plant in Alabama and ran Pasta & Cheese, an upscale food retailer in Manhattan that grew to seven outlets from one on his watch.

Buying a family business where family remains involved can often become a disaster for the vendor, the purchaser, or both. In the case of La Marzocco, the two sides now work well together, but it took time. "I've got a lot of patience. We consciously tried not to push the family out or come in and revolutionize things. I'm more of an entrepreneur, not a big business corporate guy who thinks everything goes in boxes and they all come out the same," said Cook.

Over time, Ron took charge while second-generation family member Piero Bambi oversaw research and did PR. In addition to that eventual division of duties, another decision also made a big difference. The company had opened a second plant in Seattle in 1994 solely to make machines for Starbucks until the retailing giant decided to buy only automated equipment. Cook and his fellow investors seriously considered making such machines but concluded that they would instead remain true to the handmade heritage rather than chase one customer, no matter how big. In 2004 they closed the Seattle plant and added two experienced sales representatives based in Milan. Annual production immediately jumped 40 per cent to 1,850 machines sold through forty-eight distributors in forty-two countries.

The difference between a La Marzocco machine and some of its competitors is that La Marzocco has two stainless steel boilers, one for water and one for milk, with stable temperature and steam pressure control. As a result, the machines are expensive; a model with four brewing groups and spigots retails for US$16,000. This is the high end of a huge global market in which La Marzocco occupies a tiny niche with about one-half of one per cent of all sales. Major competitors include Faema, which recently bought the other giant, Ciambli.

Ron, Jean, and their teenaged son, Charlie, live in a three-bedroom apartment near the English Cemetery. Jean plays tennis and is a volunteer assistant librarian at the American School that Charlie attends. After four years living in Florence, the couple realized that they couldn't go back, didn't want to go back, to the United States. "There might have been a moment of realization, but I think it crept up on us. When you hit the wall, and you don't bounce back to the States but keep going, that's a big milestone. Moving back to a culture a second time was actually harder than moving the first time," said Cook.

Ron considered applying for Italian citizenship in order to give Charlie an Italian passport so he'd be able to work anywhere in the European Union once he's finished school. But while they were eligible, becoming Italian citizens would have meant giving up their American citizenships, a step they did not want to take, so they will have to be satisfied with the permanent residency status that all three possess. "This is home. I want to retire here," he said.

Meanwhile, Cook sees his life as one where he has achieved self-actualization, a term he first learned from Abraham Maslow's "Hierarchy of Human Needs." Cook defines self-actualization as "the state of being content with what you're doing, content with the contribution you're making, wanting to go to work every morning, really enjoying what your life is all about." Sounds like an Italian in everything but citizenship.

Americans living in Florence are not unusual. In addition to the Cooks we met many Americans who came and stayed, including artist Robert Heylmun who lives across the street from the Pitti Palace. Canadians don't seem to have either the same wanderlust or similar willingness to pull up stakes and move to the Old World. Hundreds of OCAD students have completed the Florence program during the last thirty years but only a handful remained in Italy or returned after graduation to pursue careers. Obviously, geography and language both play a role. For Canadians who want to swim in a bigger pool, the United States offers plenty of scope and is so close at hand.

One entrepreneur who successfully straddles Italy and Canada is David Rocco. Late on a November afternoon, we're sitting in Caffè Paszkowski, drinking *cioccolata calda*, hot chocolate so thick and sweet, it might just as well be 100 per cent melted cacao, which it probably is. Rocco is showing me his hands. At fifteen, when he was growing up in Toronto, he was a male model for department store catalogs and Thrifty's, the clothing retailer. He also appeared in beer commercials and McDonald's ads. But his most lucrative work as a young man was doing hand modeling, holding items for the camera. "I made a boatload of money," he says, shaking his head at the mere memory.

Today he is a TV food show host with his own show, *David Rocco's Dolce Vita*, so his hands – how they look and what they do – remain important. Four days earlier he had an accident on the set. While slicing celery with a large chef's knife, he reached the end of the celery stalk then continued on to the index finger of his left hand, whacking off one-third of the nail and a chunk of flesh as well.

For the next shoot in the thirteen shows he's doing this year, Rocco was scheduled to go to a boys' camp forty minutes from Florence. Rather than flounder with an injured finger, or show the bandaged digit on camera, the twelve-year-olds took over and did all the cooking. Rolling his eyes at the recollection, Rocco says, "Never work with animals or children."

But Rocco can't play switcheroo every time. The TV audience wants to see him in action, so production will halt for the next two weeks while he heals. No matter, there are plenty of other things to do – scripts to write, travel arrangements to make, recipes to gather.

Rocco's shows usually involve finding fresh produce,

cheese-making, or revealing the recipes of Sicily, the Amalfi coast, or elsewhere. In Italy, there is no national cuisine. "The cooking of Italy is really the cooking of its regions, regions that until 1861 were separate, independent, and usually hostile states," says one of Italy's best-known food writers, Marcella Hazan in the introduction to *The Classic Italian Cookbook*. "Out of the abundance of the Bolognese kitchen comes cooking that is exuberant, prodigal with precious ingredients, and wholly baroque in its restless exploration of every agreeable combination of texture and flavour. The Florentine, careful and calculating, is a man who knows the measure of all things and his cooking is an austerely composed play upon essential and unadorned themes. Bologna will sauté veal in butter, stuff it with the finest mountain ham, coat it with aged Parmesan, simmer it in sauce, and smother it with the costliest truffles. Florence takes a T-bone stake of noble size and grills it quickly over the blazing fire, adding nothing but the aroma of freshly ground pepper and olive oil. Both are triumphs."

Rocco was born in Toronto and has his Economics degree from York University. His parents emigrated from Naples in 1961, ran a hairdressing salon together and taught him by example about the work ethic as well as how a couple should function in business. By the time Rocco was twenty, he'd been to Italy ten times.

David and his wife, Nina, ran a restaurant for two years before creating a travel and cooking show called *Avventura: Journeys in Italian Cuisine* that appeared on PBS in the United States as well as outlets in forty other countries.

After twenty-six episodes, the couple decided they didn't like the direction the production company was heading, so they launched their own show, *David Rocco's Dolce Vita*. In 2003–4, they shot thirteen episodes and are shooting another thirteen in 2004–5 with David as the star and Nina as executive producer. The magic number is fifty-two, four years of production at the current pace, so networks can air a show weekly for a year without a repeat. The show is broadcast in Canada on the Food Network and TLN. It has been sold to UK Food, BBC Worldwide, and also airs in France, Israel, New Zealand, and Australia.

In addition to the usual kitchen settings, there are also exteriors, dining-room scenes, and a rotating cast of more than two dozen "characters" – mostly family and friends – who participate regularly. "It's entertainment but there has to be a strong knowledge base about food and recipes. This is everyday Italian food. If an ingredient is not in season, the dish is not made. It's about assembling the ingredients; it's about passion. We hope we can inspire people to feel alive, to be spontaneous, to live more of an Italian lifestyle, to invite family and friends over just to break bread," he said.

Rocco spends four months a year based in Florence living in a family apartment near Santa Croce, scooting around the city on an electric cart. The other eight months he's in Toronto doing editing and post-production work. Each episode costs one hundred thousand dollars, with scripts and call sheets laying out a precise schedule. Three or four taping days are required to obtain enough content for the twenty-two minutes that, when surrounded by ads, fill the half-hour on-air slot. Rocco has a crew of thirteen, an expensive entourage to move around. In the past few weeks they've done shows in Positano, Ravello, and Chianti.

But the TV show is not really what David Rocco is all about. "It's like Martha Stewart. You use the show to sell the host, myself; it's all the ancillary products." And so the real focus is on marketing the maestro. David and Nina are preparing a lifestyle cookbook, creating a CD of the show's music sound-track, and seeking product endorsements. "A bad cooking show teaches you how to cook; a good cooking show inspires you how to live," says Rocco. "I'm not a chef, I'm Italian. That's my birthright, that's my mantra."

❖❖

"Stick your finger in," says my host. I stare at the thin stream of olive oil spewing from the press into a vat below. This *olio nuovo* is lime green in color, slightly cloudy, and exudes a fresh vibrancy unlike anything I have ever seen before. All I can think about is the dozen bottles of the final product that will contain a bit of me as well as nature. Still, this is an offer I can't refuse. I stick my finger in. The oil feels soft to the skin. I pull my finger away and draw the dab of oil near my nose. Smell the peppery fragrance! Taste the piquancy on the tongue! I close my eyes in wonderment. Every other olive oil seems greasy by comparison.

It is the end of November and this spicy ambrosia is being produced in Montefiridolfi, twenty kilometers south of Florence, at Villa S. Andrea, a hilltop estate that since the thirteenth century has been occupied by only a handful of families, beginning with the Buondelmontis more than one thousand years ago. Our landlord, Signor Bianchi, who brings his own grapes and olives here to be made into wine and oil, has driven Sandy and me here today and makes the introductions. Although we have talked by telephone and he has been to the apartment several times since our arrival, this is our first chance to spend much time together. A retired banker, Signor Bianchi is enthusiastic about the world around him but discreet about himself. Everything is kept on a professional level; he calls me Signor McQueen, I call him Signor Bianchi. We discover that he lives outside Florence in a town called Impruneta, but we learn little else about his personal life.

In the ten days since we visited the town of Arezzo, also in these Chianti hills, fall has arrived. Overnight frosts have wilted the geraniums but the rosemary continues to thrive. The leaves on the trees have turned yellow, and gold, and brown, all punctuated by the rows of cypress that look like exclamation points in the sentence structure of this undulating landscape.

Villa S. Andrea has six hundred hectares (about fifteen hundred acres), portions of which are planted in silver-leaved olive trees and carefully pruned grape vines all visible from the high hill where the owner's villa and production facilities are located. Roman soldiers camped on this spot two thousand years ago because of the commanding views of the valley below. During the Second World War the medieval castle standing on the site was occupied by German troops. The Allies took the hill on their march north through Italy, only to be attacked

in turn by the Germans who knew the strategic value of the location. An American cemetery nearby, a manicured expanse with rows of white crosses, bespeaks the human toll. Bullets remain embedded in a three-hundred-year-old cypress near the cantina. All that's left of the castle, destroyed by German bombing, is the vaulted stone cave where the estate's Chianti Classico wine now ages in oak casks.

"We'll follow the same path as the olives," says Leila Van Fraeijenhove, a Dutch-born employee who is showing us around. Tuscany's olive trees yield about 20 per cent of Italian production. Harvesting begins in October and lasts four to six weeks. Pickers using hand rakes comb the olives off the trees and let them fall onto tarps of a fabric that's like parachute silk lying on the ground. Not all the olives are fully ripe but everything must be picked before any fatal frost. As a result, the elongated olives range in color from light green to black. They're dumped into bins, placed on a flatbed trailer, and then pulled by tractor to the mill. At this stage, there's no time to waste. Piles of olives grow warm, like wet hay in a barn. There's no fear of fire from internal combustion, but if left untouched, the olives will ferment and be unusable. The olives are washed in a process that also removes leaves and twigs, are placed on circular mats, and then get crushed between two stones to create a brownish paste that looks like a hors d'oeuvre spread. The mats are placed on the press with a stainless steel disc inserted between every fifth mat, until the stack rises more than one hundred mats high. Under the force of the press, the oil is squeezed from the paste, drips off the edges, gets collected and then spews into a vat – the moment when I took my taste.

Olive oil is as revered as wine. It gets mixed with salad greens, poured on soups and pastas, wiped from a plate with bread, or can be used to treat dry skin or diaper rash. The ten thousand olive trees at Villa S. Andrea will produce about one hundred thousand liters of oil. This year's crop is particularly good. About 18 per cent of the olive is oil, the rest water. Some years, oil content can be as low as 14 per cent. In those years, quality remains high, but production drops. The previous year's harvest, for example, yielded seventy-five thousand liters.

The oil sits in the vat until any sediment settles and then is filtered twice through cotton for purity. Meanwhile, the mats are carried back to the starting point where the desiccated and flattened residue is scraped off and collected for resale to other producers. Villa S. Andrea only makes what's known as extra virgin, which means less than 1 per cent acidity. The lower the acid level, the longer the oil lasts before going rancid. The brown residue can be used for lower-quality and less-expensive oils such as virgin, which run about 4 per cent acidity, or to produce bottles that simply say "olive oil" without any mention of extra virgin or virgin. "The other is not what you want to make," says Leila. "You focus on the quality products and you remain with that."

Such attention to quality – the handmade espresso machines of La Marzocco or olive oil from Villa S. Andrea – is a hallmark of many Italian producers. Most of the better-known designer clothing and leather labels have refused to move production of luxury goods to low-cost Asian factories, preferring instead to continue making their items in Italy where there is a tradition of care and the capacity to maintain quality control.

Retailers follow similar proud practices. If you buy two tarts at the pasticceria to take home for dessert, the packaging takes longer than the selection process. The items are set on doilies in a hard cardboard tray that has raised and scalloped edges with a strip of cardboard that's bent and formed into a C-shaped curve then tucked underneath at both tray ends to create a protective arch. The whole ensemble is wrapped in paper bearing the shop's name and address, taped, and then tied with colorful ribbon and a decorative bow.

As we get ready to leave Villa S. Andrea, Leila stops at a wall where a Roman sentry likely stood guard, points to a building across the valley, and says, "They buy what we throw away." When she tells me the company's name, it sounds familiar. Sure enough, the olive oil in our kitchen, bought a few weeks back when I was young and naïve about these matters, was from the second-rate place. What I bought, I now throw away.

DECEMBER

BEYOND THE HIGH-RENT HISTORIC CENTER of Florence where tourists gawk, there's a different streetscape. On every block, there is at least one artisan, visible through a window, working away in a tiny shop: a bookbinder with a bowed head stitching pages together, a violin maker lovingly polishing a piece of wood, two men carving fluted adornments for furniture and fireplace mantels.

The money can't be much but their work, carried out in the same manner for centuries, is honored in the community. On Via dell'Agnolo, Carlo Saitta operates in two rooms so humble that most North Americans would think twice before using them as storage space. But in these confined quarters he makes beautiful marbleized paper using a time-honored method that combines the cadence of tai chi with the artistry of Jackson Pollock.

Inside the front door to the right, an antique paper press of mammoth proportions dominates the shop's front room. To the left are displays of his work: jewelry trays, notebooks with leather spines, and keepsake boxes with satin-ribbon pulls, all decorated with the richness of his handmade marbleized paper in various color combinations: blues and gold, reds and purple, greens and yellow. While marbleized or decorated paper was probably invented in China, it has been produced in Italy since the fifteenth century, and is used as clothing in *The Adventures of Pinocchio*, when Collodi says, "Geppetto, who was poor and hadn't even a cent in his pocket, made him a little suit of flowered paper."

A narrow corridor leads to a step down, another step up, and into a well-lit workshop where there's barely enough space for a visitor to watch while Carlo weaves his magic. He is a happy apple dumpling of a man who does not look anything like his sixty-six years. His dark eyes sparkle, his wrinkle-free face is as smooth as a baby's skin, his black hair lies flat on his scalp, and a boyish cowlick spills across his brow. He wears a navy work coat and his feet are planted firmly apart at his waist-high workbench as if he's ready for a sea voyage. Above the bench located in a corner of the room, the speckled paint on the walls from previous years could be modern art suitable for framing.

On top of the bench sits a rectangular metal tray that measures about 50 x 75 cm, two-thirds filled with water. He adds dollops of liquid starch, stirs the gelatinous ingredients vigorously with a stick until he has a thick emulsion, and then removes surface bubbles by skimming the liquid with the thin edge of a flat board. Beside the tray sit metal containers that hold plastic glasses, each containing a different color of paint. This morning he is working with dark blue, light blue, and gold. With his left hand, he thrusts the tip of a small brush into the dark blue paint, and then holds the brush above the pan, with the paint poised and pregnant. He takes in his right hand a wooden device that's shaped like the hand bell once used to summon schoolchildren. He taps the middle of the wand on the narrow neck of the "bell" so that droplets of paint fall from the brush into the liquid below. When the drops hit the surface of the bath, they expand and form a series of small circles. As the tapping continues at a steady pace, Carlo moves the wand from left to right, right to left, back and forth, all the while drawing the wand toward the other end of the pan to ensure even distribution. The careful process is repeated with the other two colors, light blue and gold, with each successive spattering process carried out closer to the tray. Surface tension keeps each drop and all the colors separate. He waits for a minute, watching the droplets as they form small spots and larger circles, looking for secret signs only known to an artisan who has done this procedure thousands of times.

When his instinct tells him that the moment for the next step arrives, he pokes a short round stick into the solution and, using a quick zigzag motion, creates a colorful pattern of narrow, parallel lines. Next he picks up a piece of wood that's as long as the pan is wide. From the device sprout fine wire tines, each about four centimeters long, all arranged closely together in a single row. He holds the tool in both hands and deftly skims the surface with the wire tips, working in a wavy motion, all the while drawing the tool toward him. When he has traveled the length of the pan, he lifts the tool, wipes the wire ends clean with a sponge, and then skims the surface again, this time working across the width to create a pleasing series of tri-colored patterns.

Carlo replaces the first wire tool with another similar device that has two staggered rows of wire tines set further apart. He repeats the skimming and wiping process, rocking back and forth while maintaining constant contact between the tips and the liquid's surface to achieve a series of small, shell-like shapes.

Now Carlo must transfer that luxurious look to paper. He takes from a nearby stack a piece of yellow paper that's slightly smaller than the tray, lays it gently on the liquid so that the paper floats on the surface, and leaves it just long enough to allow the paper to absorb some of the paint. He then rests a small square-shaped wooden stick on the end of the tray and pulls the paper toward him, drawing it through the narrow opening between the stick and the tray edge. The paper comes out "printed" with the colors adhering to the underside, a per-fect match for surface pattern. He flips the paper over and sets it on a board in a drying rack behind him, wet side up. He wipes any paint residue from the tray's edge and, with another piece of paper, repeats that final step until the rack is filled with papers, each slightly different than the rest.

Silently he works, moving with the adept grace of a ballet star following a tempo that appears to be set internally by his very heartbeat. There are no intrusive noises, just the tapping of the wooden brush on the mallet, the gentle patter as the paint drops, and the modest rustle of paper. The entire process creates a zen-like state where man and paint and paper are united as if they are one.

Indeed, Carlo could be a monk in the Middle Ages doing illuminated manuscripts. He may not have taken religious vows, but he demands as little for himself from this life as does a man of the cloth. All that he needs is close at hand amid the haphazard piles of leather skins that, with the marbleized paper, go into the finished goods he sells.

Common elements are beginning to emerge among the happiest people in Florence. Antonio the waiter, Bettina the painter, Carlo the marbleizer – all share a dedication to excellence through the dexterity of their own hands. Using their God-given talents to do work with inherent value brings a contentment that can only come from a job well done rather than giving in to the rat race for material goods that at the end of the day don't matter much anyway. At the same time, they are granted a respected place in this society because this city has a tradition of honoring the work of the artisan rather than worshipping some bond trader who just makes money in mysterious ways.

After three months of living in Florence, you get to thinking: Why not extend the fantasy? Why not stay here permanently? It's not that we think we know the place so well as to be able to make that decision, but we have moved somewhere beyond being mere tourists. We arrived in this different zone very quickly on the second night by taking part in the parade with lanterns, but have we moved along far enough to take up full-time residence?

Luigi Barzini's thoughtful book, *The Italians*, first published in 1964, gives fair warning to foreigners who think they can decipher the puzzling Italian psyche. "Italy is universally considered a particularly unpredictable and deceptive country. Some people even believe that this is the only absolutely certain thing about it. They are, of course, right some of the time, but also wrong as often. There are no sure guides to what Italy is and what it might do next. Italians themselves are almost always baffled by their own behavior. The only people who have no doubts and hold very definite and clear ideas about the country and its inhabitants are foreigners who streak through it in a few days," wrote Barzini.

German sociologist Hans Magnus Enzensberger was even more definitive in his 1990 book *Europe, Europe* when he said, "The Germans, the English or the Finns could not act like the Italians even if they wanted to. They're not astute enough, not cynical enough, not talented enough; they're too stubborn, too set in their ways, too amateurish, too inhibited. They've invested too much energy in their well-ordered systems, delegated too many resources, responsibilities, and hopes to the state. They're out of practice when it comes to relying on their own initiative and can't say, 'Me and my clan, my family, my shop, we'll manage – and all the rest can go to hell.'"

To find out if a recently arrived couple like us could live

here permanently I seek advice from Carol Milligan. Carol is an American with a Canadian father, John Milligan, a Shakespearean actor now living in Alabama. Carol moved to Florence at fifteen with her mother, stepfather, and family in 1973. Now forty-eight, she has been active in the local real estate market in one way or another for twenty-five years. She attended American and Italian high schools in Florence and then graduated from an Italian university where she was hired as housing director to oversee student accommodation.

In 1989, she and her sister Kirste decided to open their own rental agency, Milligan & Milligan, to help students, holidayers, and convention delegates find short-term apartments. Most Florentines in a similar start-up would rent office space, buy a truckload of equipment, open their doors, and hope for the best. "It's like when Italians do sports. You buy all the possible equipment and then see if you like it," she says. Carol followed the more traditional practice of women in Canada and the United States by launching a home-based business in order to keep costs down. Her previous contact with landlords, along with word of mouth, meant that the company flourished. The partnership, however, did not. Two sisters in business is often a difficult dynamic and Kirste soon left. By 1991, Carol had built the business to the point where she felt she was able to rent space, buy equipment and furniture, and hire an assistant. Within weeks George Bush launched the Gulf War, causing values in the local housing market to fall by 20 per cent, but Milligan pressed on regardless and was one of the first firms to reach prospects using the Internet. Today her business is a balance of vacation rentals for people from many nations as well as buyers – mostly from the United States, Canada, and Australia – looking to live in Tuscany.

Of all the regions of Italy, Tuscany is among the most expensive. A one-bedroom apartment in central Florence in a building with an elevator (only 10 per cent of apartments have them) costs about 500,000 euros or C\$800,000. A sweeping city view near Piazzale Michelangelo, halfway up the hill to San Miniato al Monte, will cost 1 million euros and will likely be part of a larger villa. Properties on the way to Fiesole, also with excellent views, are priced somewhere in between. House prices, stable for a long time, have quadrupled in the last five years.

A villa in the countryside, with ten or fifteen rooms, that once housed a feudal lord and all his servants, will start at 1 million euros and require an unpredictable amount of money if updating has not already been done. Because everything is built of stone, including the internal walls, modernizing the wiring or the plumbing means a sledgehammer followed by stonemasons. "In Florence, you can turn off the water in a building from the 1400s and some apartments may still have running water because they're attached somewhere else to what was once a monastery and you don't know where the water main is. You open up a wall, find some old terra cotta tiles, and you don't know what they're for. Are they still in use or not? You never know what you're going to find. Even something small is a very big job." All exterior renovations must be in keeping with history. You can't knock down an old building to erect a new dream house.

For the sake of argument, let's settle on buying a former barn in the Tuscan countryside with an asking price of 600,000 euros. Best bet is to hire an English- and Italian-speaking agent as your *mandatario* who will represent you and be paid only by you. Closing the deal is a process that is lengthy, bureaucratic, and requires telling a few white lies along the way. The first stage is called the *preliminare* when you make an offer of, say, 550,000 euros accompanied by a down-payment check for 50,000 euros. Finding a notary to handle the matter takes two weeks and organizing a mortgage with the bank might take a month. If the owner accepts the offer, he has six months to find another place to live. During the next few weeks, if the buyer backs out, the owner keeps the deposit. If the owner decides to sell to someone else, he pays the maker of the first offer twice the deposit as a penalty for taking a higher price.

The second stage is the *compromesso*, the promissory contract. The buyer adds another 50,000 euros to firm up the deal. Now come the lies of Pinocchio proportions. The actual sale price will not be registered with the *catasto*, the registry office. The *catasto* has already established an official value upon which property taxes are based. For a house in the 500,000-euros price range, this authorized number could be as low as 140,000 euros. Once the buyer and seller agree on the sale price then they also agree on another much lower price that will be submitted to the *catasto*. As long as that declared price is slightly higher than the official price, even as little as 1,000 euros higher, everyone is satisfied, and the process keeps moving along. The *compromesso* is supposed to take place in the presence of notaries for both sides, but the notaries usually stay away. They don't want any part of that hanky-panky for fear of court proceedings later when they might have to testify.

The third and final stage, the *rogito*, or final contract, may not occur until a year after the offer was first made. On this occasion the notaries do attend, along with the buyer and seller, in order to conclude the deal, make sure there are no liens against the property, and certify that all previous renovations have been approved by the local municipality. Many people don't bother seeking official consent for such work, knowing that every few years there's a sweeping pardon anyway. The deed is transferred and the sale registered at the phony price.

The notary, who is fully complicit in the false filing, charges his fee based on an entirely different amount, somewhere between the registered price and real price. Depending on your facility in Italian and the amount of work involved, the agency charges anywhere from 2 to 6 per cent of the same number. This under-the-table culture has developed because the modern state is fairly recent. "We have Italy, now we need Italians," said Massimo D'Azeglio around the time the country was founded in 1870. To a great extent that need remains. "Until then, every single little town – mainly run by the Church – had its own rules and customs," says Milligan. "That has pretty much stuck. Italy is not easy to change. What has happened is that some ways of doing things are still very feudal. Italians still work very much on a family clan society. It's not a government society."

"A lot of people, especially in the poor areas down south, feel that they give a lot of money and get nothing back. There has been a lot of corruption, which has spread into many other areas where the people are fairly well to do. It's very different from our [North American] part of the world and I can't say one is right and the other is wrong, it's just different. That's the strange thing about living overseas so long. You can see the way the people think in the countries where you live but you still understand how the people think where you come from and you're not really totally one or totally the other."

When it comes to housing, there are two distinct Florences: the medieval downtown and the post-war suburbs. In the historic center of Florence, the streets are relatively narrow, twisting, and designed to give tourists the slip. There's beauty at every turn: a column topped by a statue or a portrait of Mary and the Christ child behind glass, placed there by a local family hundreds of years earlier. Look up and see painted wall patterns, wrought-iron railings, and leering gargoyles. Look down and see cobblestones, ancient metal plates, and helter-skelter sewers that go who-knows-where.

In the eastern reaches of Florence, the medieval may have been replaced by the modern, but there is splendor in the grass, parks with trees, geraniums in gardens, and shrubbery-lined sidewalks. The leaves on the magnolia grandiflora are so shiny you'd think someone had wiped each of them individually with balls of cotton batten dipped in milk. Even the standard-issue three-storey apartment buildings are proudly painted a brilliant yellow and feature balconies with succulents and cacti, lovingly tended. There are also towering palms and pomegranate trees laden with ripened fruit. The skins have split open to reveal the ruby red seeds inside. Blackbirds have taken up residence, their meals assured.

Several hundred of us have gathered outside the local community center, awaiting the noon opening of the annual Christmas bazaar. The iron gate is closed, guarded by ladies wearing badges that say Bazaar Helper, as the rest of us start rhythmic clapping at ten minutes to twelve. It's hard to imagine grown men and women this eager to paw through donated items or buy goodies at a bake table, but here we are, slavering to see what's on sale.

When noon finally arrives, the gate slides open, and we surge ahead twelve abreast toward a door that can admit but two at a time. All the legions of Rome could not stop our forward advancement. Within fifteen minutes the rooms on all three floors are clogged with shoulder-to-shoulder buyers at every table. Security guards halt passage on staircases until other shoppers leave the upstairs rooms, making space for those who patiently wait their turn.

This is the annual Christmas Bazaar sponsored by the American International League of Florence Onlus. Onlus means non-profit; all the proceeds go to charity. The event began as a bazaar in a church basement but has grown so large over the years that it has moved three times to larger premises. This location looks ready to be replaced, too.

On the main floor there's vintage jewelry, beads, brooches, and earrings for two to five euros. A bake table offers homemade cookies, cakes, tea breads, and preserves, similarly priced. Across the room are a few higher-ticket items: two leather chairs at 150 euros each and a gilded frame for 200 euros. Downstairs are racks of second-hand men's and women's clothing as well as accessories: scarves, handbags, belts, and capes. Upstairs are children's toys, games, and stuffed animals.

A trip for two to New York is first prize in the lucky draw, but there are also fifty prizes from Ferragamo. The organization asked for one prize and the designer donated two large boxes filled with scarves and weekend bags. Outside, hamburgers and hotdogs sizzle on the barbecue. Also available are bowls of the traditional Florentine peasant soup, *ribollita*, made with stale bread, beans, and a local leafy variety of kale called *cavolo nero*. But there's another indication that this event could only be taking place in Italy. The sign listing prices has soft drinks at 1.50, bottled water for 1 euro, and a glass of wine for half a euro.

Among the attendees is Ron Cook, of La Marzocco, the espresso machine maker. He's outside, keeping a watchful eye on the Weber barbecues being used to broil the hamburgers. He'll be borrowing those barbecues the following week for the annual employee Christmas party held at his plant. This year, there will be a change in the menu. Five of his employees at La Marzocco are Muslims, so in addition to the traditional Florentine beef specialty, *bistecca*, he's also cooking goat meat, making hummus, and supplying pita bread. "This is the new Italy," he says. "Time to get in step." A few days ago, in Rome, there were footsteps of a different sort as hundreds who oppose immigration angrily marched in the streets carrying banners that said, "Muslims go home." I prefer Ron's way of walking.

Christmas has also arrived on Via Roma and the rest of the pedestrian area around our apartment. Dozens of four-foot-high cedar trees in terra cotta planters have been set out on the sidewalks, tucked against the buildings. The rows of trees, placed between shop windows, stretch in all directions as far as the eye can see. Once in place, each is trimmed with fairy lights.

Every street also has its own slightly different version of strings of lights on high, but they're all white, so they seem to be of a piece. Some look like waterfalls, others form rolling waves, a third type rises to a series of peaks like a Gothic vault. Signs saying *Buon Natale* are everywhere, but a White Christmas is unlikely. When snow does fall here, it usually doesn't last very long.

Storefronts, hung with garlands of branches, flowers, and fruit, look like Luca Della Robbia ceramics. At Coin, one of Italy's major department stores, wreaths and beribboned boxes dangle in the atrium. Churches give over entire altars to local artists who create *presipio* that can be quite elaborate. These manger scenes can measure up to four meters square with fig-ures showing the Holy Family and the adoration of the shepherds and Wise Men. The creations often include the sur-rounding desert's scrubby trees as well as mountains with sheep and goats.

Street vendors are in sync with the season. The Asian

women who usually sell shawls are offering two types of head-gear: red Santa hats with flashing lights or clip-on reindeer antlers. Buskers play seasonal music, hoping the Christmas spirit includes them. Unlike in Canada, where slow retail sales might spark early discounts, by government decree such reductions cannot start until January 7.

In the midst of all the seasonal change, one aspect of Florentine life remains constant: the daily parade. On the first Sunday of the month that day's event is announced by the tooting of klaxons and the roar of engines as a convoy of about one hundred Fiat 500 cars arrive and park higgledy-piggledy in the open space west of the Baptistery. Riding herd are a dozen men on Harley-Davidson motorcycles wearing orange fluorescent vests announcing themselves as Road Captains, presumably one giant step up in authority from Road Warriors.

Viewed from our window, the Fiats with their fabric sunroofs form a pattern that reminds me of the plaque on the base of the statute of Ferdinand I in the Piazza Santissima Annunziata. Showing a Queen bee surrounded by five circles of worker bees, *"Maiestate tantum"* states the inscription, "In between many, there is only one." In this case the one is a British-built Morgan in classic silver, surrounded by the Italian Fiat 500s in white, yellow, red, dark blue, gray, and various shades of orange-brown, all with sporty sunroofs of tarp or glass.

The *cinquecento* (cheen-kway-**chen**-toe), as the Fiat is universally and lovingly known, is to Italy what the Morris Minor is to England or the Volkswagen Beetle to Germany – the people's car. Introduced in 1957, the Fiat looks no bigger than the bubble in a pond created by a frog's fart. Built to allow workers more freedom to find jobs farther afield, the last *cinquecento* came off the assembly line thirty years ago but of the more than 3.5 million built, some six hundred thousand are still on the road, a miracle of metallic longevity.

Lately the *cinquecento* has come under fire. The rear-mounted engine has no catalytic converter so does not meet modern-day emission standards. In response, an emotional outcry has risen from those who fondly remember the *cinquecento* as an integral part of the 1960s sexual revolution. When the pill arrived and the Catholic Church began losing its power, the *cinquecento* offered a place – albeit cramped – for sex out of sight of prying parental eyes.

This celebratory parade, sponsored by the Fiat Club of Firenze, has little to do with green causes. The owners are simply members of a community of like-minded souls who are showing off their restoration handiwork and drawing nostalgic admiration as they motor from place to place. After thirty minutes, with much unnecessary revving of engines, they're gone. Amid the departing cacophony of horns, one delivers a few bars from "Oh Susanna," a popular song from another land in another time. Not to be outdone, a few weeks later, more than one hundred Minis and Mini-Coopers, many with Union Jacks painted on their roofs, thunder through the same area but do not deign to stop.

Unseasonably mild weather, which makes such outdoor events and parades so enjoyable, continues well into December.

We sit outside for lunch at Gilli, a café that moved to Piazza della Repubblica in 1910 but has been a fixture in Florence since 1733. The awnings that shaded diners a few months ago have been rolled back against the wall, and the number of linen-covered tables has shrunk by more than half, but at 20°C in full sun, this mid-month experience is that much more enjoyable because the pleasure seems somehow stolen from the weather gods. On the left side of the piazza is the Hotel Savoy where rooms start at four hundred U.S. dollars a night. On the far side, vendors sell leather goods from carts that are rolled away nightly and there's a restaurant that tries to trade on its past glories as a place where writers once gathered. On the right, under an arcade, are flower stalls, newsstands, and a bookshop. A group of twenty retired men meet daily near the taxi stand, gesticulating emphatically, as they all talk at once about soccer, politics, other times, other days. A string quartet plays Vivaldi, the hopeful hat on the pavement mostly empty of donated coins at this time of year. A tricked-out pair of tourists in their thirties ambles by, he in a ball cap, she wearing a belt with a gold buckle. His cap, her belt, and his shirt are each emblazoned with the same word: RICH. All cannot live on the piazza, goes the Italian proverb, but everyone can enjoy the sun.

❧

After three months, the first semester is over. We gather with Sandy's fellow students on a Thursday night for wine and pizza at Trattoria da Garabardi, near the San Lorenzo leather market. Huddled in a corner are four students from another program, all slope-shouldered and sad-eyed. They head home tomorrow, their time in Italy at an end. The OCAD students occupy a long table in the middle of the room and are boisterous by comparison. They're less than halfway along; ahead lies the second term and many more discoveries. They spend the evening eating, drinking, and drawing each other on the paper placemats. These are "blind" sketches where the artist cannot look at what she's creating and must not lift the pencil from the paper until the work is completed. The graphic renditions can be quite telling. The most prominent feature of a face or the inner personality is often captured – or caricatured – with deadly accuracy.

All that remains of this term is the final art history exam and the student exhibit when the nineteen students show off their creativity. Teacher Laura Millard met with groups of students each week, offering commentary and criticism about their work. At these critiques, or "crits" as they are called, other students also state their opinions. But this is a self-directed program, so for the most part, everyone is on his or her own to find inspiration and apply perspiration.

Given so much freedom, some are flourishing while others flounder. Many, in their early twenties, are away from home for the first time. A few are homesick and lost in the new culture, some party too much, and others have no self-imposed work ethic so their body of work is slim. The favorite word is *sketchy*, a fitting remark for artists to sprinkle throughout conversations. You feel sketchy or lacking in confidence, your work is sketchy or uncompleted, someone else is sketchy or not to be trusted, plans for the weekend are sketchy . . . you get the idea. The most favorite expletive seems to be *snot*. Snot is the new fuck. Second place goes to *vomit*.

Sarah Todd is taking a double major at OCAD that includes curatorial studies, so she has been appointed curator of the exhibit. It's a powerful role that means she picks what to include from the student sculptures, installations, drawings, painting, photography, and performance art and then decides where everything will be displayed in the hallways and eight studios that make up the space. Todd has entitled the show *Infinito*. "We are unfinished in many ways, we have not yet completed our formal education, and we are not fully formed as artists. *Infinito* is about recognizing the possibility in the incomplete," she says in her curatorial statement. "Making contemporary art in a city so obsessed with its past has produced friction and the finite amount of time we are here has created pressure. *Infinito* is the other shoe falling, the transitory public event that documents the evidence of three months' living and working in Florence. *Infinito* is recognizing that 'right now there is a moment of time passing by – we must become that moment,'" she says, quoting French painter Paul Cezanne.

The most compelling work is Andrew Waite's roomful of two-meter-tall corn stalks made of aluminum foil, each suspended by fishing wire from the ceiling, waving in the breeze caused by a small electric fan. A meandering pathway allows the viewer to plunge amidst the rustling leaves and be transported elsewhere. First-rate paintings by Bill Kreznarich and Raf Zawistowski could hang in any gallery. Maryam Keyhani's mixed media chandeliers use innovative materials, including red wine, as a way of allowing her to question the use of alcohol – something prohibited in her ancient culture of Iran.

My vote for best in show goes, of course, to Sandy's three wire-sculpture dresses – *The Three Graces*. Created using various types of wire and then decorated with beads, semi-precious stones, pearls, and found objects, each dress hangs by a slender strand of silver wire and casts a playful shadow on the wall. Local artist Romano Morando praises Sandy's compositions as "angelic," recalling a time of innocence that was long ago lost. Morando says that her use of light has inspired him to apply more light in his own work. "I am a painter of the shadow. You are the sun," he says.

When the show is over we carry the dresses home, thereby producing another parade through the streets of Florence that attracts interest from passersby who are curious about the creations floating along. We hang all three ladies from the blades of the ceiling fan. Suspended at different heights in the middle of the living room, they take on a life of their own, as if they are dancing to the music of the spheres.

During our first few months we've visited Prato, Siena, Arezzo, Bologna, and many other nearby towns and cities, but there's no need to leave Florence to have a day trip. There's always a wonderful exhibit at the Pitti Palace. The Boboli Gardens includes a long climb but boasts a beautiful view and ceramics gallery at the top of the hill. The Bargello Museum is filled with the world's best Renaissance sculpture, including my favorite piece in all of Florence, Donatello's bronze *David*, the first free-standing sculpture since Roman times, showing the naked and androgynous young warrior victorious, his sandaled left foot on Goliath's severed head. Many visitors wait longer in line than they actually spend in the Uffizi Gallery. Longer-term residents like us have the luxury of going in off-peak periods, stopping after two hours when the brain overflows, and returning a few weeks later to pick up where we left off.

But even if you're in Florence only for a few days, here's my advice: Don't stand in a long line up for anything. Book ahead or don't bother. Better to spend your time dreamily sipping wine in a sunlit piazza than standing behind someone from Dallas who wants to see *David* because she already bought the kitchen apron. Others make the mistake of queuing for the Duomo before opening time only to discover that it's big and beautiful but mostly empty. All the best statuary from the Duomo and the Baptistery is in the Museo dell'Opera behind the cathedral. Among the masterpieces there is a *Pietà* by Michelangelo and Donatello's *Mary Magdalene*, carved from poplar and haunting in her sunken-eyed gauntness after fasting and abstinence.

We're spending two weeks in Canada at Christmas, so for my last local visit before our departure I choose Giotto's Campanile. For all these months I have listened to the sweet sounds, but have yet to climb to the top and take a closer look. The Campanile is actually the bell tower of the Duomo, but as is typical in Italian architecture, it was built as a separate structure, rather than as part of the cathedral itself. Designed in the fourteenth century by Giotto di Bondone, only the foundation and first storey of the Gothic tower were finished by the time of his death in 1337. Giotto was an artist, not an engineer, and the builders soon realized that if they completed his plans, the structure might fall over, so they doubled the thickness of the lower walls to hold the weight. The redesign succeeded; more than five hundred years later, the Campanile's still standing.

The exterior of the slender tower is clad in the same three colors of marble as the Duomo: pink, green, and white. It is decorated with reliefs by Donatello, Luca della Robbia, and Andrea Pisano. Original sin is represented at the base; at the pinnacle, divine grace. In between are three sets of arched windows that permit the sounds of the bells to roll out across the city.

George Eliot, the nineteenth-century British novelist who researched her novel *Romola* while visiting Florence, wrote vividly of the Campanile. "The mercurial barber seized the arm of the stranger, and led him to a point, on the south side of the piazza, from which he could see at once the huge dark shell of the cupola, the slender soaring grace of Giotto's campanile . . . its harmonious variety of colour and form led the eyes upward, high into the clear air of this April morning, it seemed a prophetic symbol, telling that human life must somehow and some time shape itself into accord with that pure aspiring beauty."

The 414 steps don't seem nearly as difficult as the treads of Brunelleschi's dome. These steps are wider and there is plenty of head room as well as space for people to pass by on the way back down. At the top I stare at the terrace where Signor Bianchi took us that first day we arrived. The three months has sped by in a blink. Yet as I look around, I realize how familiar are the surroundings, how many streets and structures, palazzos and piazzas I can name. There is still much to explore, but we have seen and learned an amazing amount. I walk down one flight of steps to an open landing where a set of bells hangs and wait for them to come to life as they always do at this time of day. The process begins with a whirring and clicking of gears and pulleys and ropes. The largest bell, which is two meters across and has a clapper the size of a man's arm, begins to swing above me. This close, the sound is almost deafening. My chest becomes a vibrating part of the acoustical box, my body is all a-tingle as far down as my toes – the overall feeling is absolutely orgiastic. After a few minutes, the tolling ceases, the clapper continues to swing noiselessly on its own for a while after the bell stops reverberating. Now that I have seen this bell up close, one among the many that I have so often stopped what I was doing and listened to, I feel like we have at last been properly introduced.

The bar at the Four Seasons Yorkville is not Gilli in the noonday sun but on a snowy December day in Toronto it will do very nicely. Whatever the country, people-watching is an Olympic sport. At this cocktail hour, the best sighting is of Matthew Barrett, former chairman and CEO of Bank of Montreal, and now chairman of Barclay's in Britain. He joins two former colleagues who arrived early to secure the appropriate see-and-be-seen table. A few minutes later there is a flurry at the doorway as a woman in her thirties, wearing a luxe brocade jacket, appears. She strides toward Barrett and his acolytes with the flowing black-haired good looks of a woman who is not from these parts. After she's seated, she and Matt bill and coo a bit.

On our way out, we stop by their table to pay our respects. Barrett introduces us to Serena. When we say we're living in Florence, Serena perks up and asks where. When she hears Via Roma she says she knows Luisa Via Roma, the upscale shop in our building, perhaps not a surprising piece of fashion lore given Barrett's penchant for squiring young European beauties with expensive tastes. He is his usual self: suave, charming, and entertaining. He has enjoyed executive success at two banks in two countries. Even so, Matt Barrett momentarily exudes an aura of sadness. "Florence," he sighs. "You need a woman to go to Florence with." Despite her specific local knowledge, Serena is apparently not such a woman. I am a lucky man. Not only do I have a woman to go to Florence with, she took me.

While visiting Canada we give Christmas gifts from Italy. In a large cardboard box in the hold of the plane we brought one of the wire dress sculptures Sandy created to hang from the ceiling above the crib of Molly, our first grandchild, born into this world while we were away. There's also a lacy dress for her from Florence's finest children's clothing shop, Loretta Caponi, hand-embroidered by seamstresses working out the back. Other gifts include Ferragamo silk ties for son Mark, leather gloves for his wife Andrea, and amber earrings of dainty design for our daughter Alison. For friends there are silk scarves purchased at Cascine, the outdoor Tuesday market with two kilometer-long rows of stalls along the river, olive oil from Villa S. Andrea, and notebooks covered with marbleized paper from Carlo Saitta. We show photos to friends and try to explain how much Italy has already come to mean to us, but at home we are suddenly different. In familiar surroundings, we revert to acting like the caricatures of ourselves that people have come to expect. "In Florence," Sandy sighs, "just being me is good enough."

The streets of Florence are not safe on New Year's Eve. Gangs of youths run amok, tossing firecrackers indiscriminately into crowds. Residents throw empty bottles from their windows. Rome, they say, is even worse. Such mayhem keeps the rest of us indoors. No matter, we usually spend New Year's Eve at home anyway. We enjoyably spend the day foraging in our favorite haunts for a celebratory dinner. Cheeses, nuts, olives, and a salmon spread from the Central Market, bread and rolls from Verrazzano on Via dei Tavolini, a small pork roast from Sandro Polleria on Via dei Cerchi, rosemary, carrots, zucchini, and Sicilian cherry tomatoes from the nearby fruit and vegetable vendor, live lobster from Pescheria Alfredo on Borgo degli Albizi, and for dessert, *fedora* from Pasticceria Nencioni on Via Pietrapiana.

French pastries are generally better than Italian, but *fedora* is bar none the best dessert I've ever tasted. A combination of rum-soaked cake and whipped cream, it's all encased in dark chocolate curls. There's a hearty Chianti Classico from Villa S. Andrea, where we visited, and Lis Neris, a smooth Pinot Grigio from Friuli in the north where the best Italian whites are produced. As a digestif, Limoncello from Sorrento.

We invite Erminia Luschi, a newfound friend, to join us. Born in Salzburg, Austria, Erminia moved to Florence in 1958 when she was eighteen. In those days, the talented Erminia had her own creative career. She illustrated children's books, using pen-and-ink in powerful drawings, some of which were two-page spreads. She also did props and costumes for local theater and worked as a designer for Salvatore Ferragamo.

More recently, however, her life has not been her own. Her husband, who came from an old Florentine family, fell ill when he was in his forties. Erminia gave up her career to look after him full-time until he died. Hardly was her husband gone but her father died, and then for twenty years she nursed her ailing mother who finally died in 2003 at the age of one hundred. "I was sent to look after people. That's what I was put on this earth to do." When Erminia utters the words, she sounds neither reluctant nor resentful; she is simply stating a fact of her life.

Because her mother was so sick, there were few visitors. As a result, we were the first guests to be invited for dinner at her apartment in years. The décor is elegant and restrained. Walls and upholstery are done in white to show off her art. Fine furniture includes an ancient chest wrapped in healing cloths to fight wormwood. Her dozens of books require no index. She can rise from her chair, walk directly to a specific shelf, and put her hand on the collected works of any artist or luminary under discussion.

In her studio is an architect's drafting board and a long table on adjustable legs where she has spent too little time of late. Other than food shopping and a brief evening walk, Erminia had no free time for herself during all those caregiving years. For the eighteen months since her mother's death, she has been consumed by grief. We feel as if we were sent here to help her rejoin the world around and rejoice in life again.

We have New Year's Eve dinner at our library table in the living room with the sounds of cherry bombs wafting up from below. At one point we look out and watch a young man in a blue coat drop a firecracker into a beer bottle containing some type of flammable fluid and toss the concoction into the piazza. His hand has already suffered a severe burn, an injury that will not register in his alcohol-addled brain until tomorrow.

After dinner, we stare at the stack of dirty dishes and decide to inaugurate the dishwasher. Erminia, who has a similar apparatus, helps decipher the instructions. We have all had a tad too much to drink. After a period of silence while reading the multi-lingual booklet, she announces, "Start is an important button." We add soap, push some buttons, and amazingly, it works. There is a sudden panic when Erminia can't find her reading glasses and worries they mistakenly went in with the dishes. While I'm trying to figure out how to interrupt the washing process or shut off the contraption, she finds them. "Too much Limoncello," she laughingly concludes. We retire to the living room and talk of hopes, dreams, and aspirations for the New Year.

If I have one wish for 2005, it is to be more like the Italians. As Canadians, we are too reserved, our shoulders hunched to the ears and chins tucked into the chest as if trying to fend off winter's cold even during the summer. People are affected by their weather, so Italy is a freer place because there is less huddling. But beyond such external forces, whether they be creative artisans or caregiving relatives, Italians know who they are, revel in their talents, enjoy the beauty in which they live, and respect the roles of others.

Canada's splendor is mostly in the landscape. We do not have the creativity of the Middle Ages all around us to admire. In our cities there may be less beauty to behold, but we take too little time to enjoy the sights that do exist. As for our own lives, many people prefer to run faster as if trying to escape themselves. As that personal pace quickens, civility shrivels.

One scene from Christmas in Toronto will suffice. An old friend spotted us walking in a residential neighborhood one morning and stopped his car to say hello. As we exchanged greetings the thorougfare was blocked by the combination of me leaning into the passenger window and his car in the one-way street. When two vehicles pulled up behind him, both drivers immediately began honking their horns. I told my friend to pull onto the sidewalk in order to make room and then motioned what was happening to the drivers whose passage had been momentarily delayed.

We were not fast enough for them. The first driver, a woman at the wheel of a Lincoln Navigator, gritted her capped teeth, gunned her engine, and roared past as if she were driving a getaway car. My friend was still easing his vehicle forward and I hadn't yet had time to move off the street, so the SUV almost side-swiped me as it fish-tailed down the snowy street, slewing dangerously close to the row of parked cars. If the first woman was angry, the second was apoplectic. This glowering matron – decked out in a wide-brimmed hat and mink coat at eleven in the morning – paused on the way by, powered down her Town Car window, and shouted, "Can't you find a better place to park?" Angry Toronto women of a certain age, meet the mean young men of New Year's Eve in Florence. You have all too much in common.

JANUARY

IN THE ROMAN CATHOLIC CHURCH, **January 6 is the feast of** Epiphany, commemorating the day that the three wise men arrived with their gifts for the Christ child. For Italian children Epiphany has become a more important occasion than Christmas because this is when La Befana visits. According to legend, the three wise men asked a housewife named Befana for directions. She couldn't help and declined their invitation to join them in their quest. After the wise men left, Befana realized her missed opportunity and tried to catch up. When she failed to find them, she gave treats to every child she saw in the hopes that one of them was Christ. In modern times, Befana is still looking for the Christ child. On Epiphany she fills the stockings hung by the chimney of good children or leaves a lump of coal for those who have been bad. Befana, who is portrayed as a witch, can also be a derogatory term for any woman over thirty.

I thought the 150th anniversary of the municipal police a few weeks back was a splendid celebration, but compared with

Epiphany that earlier event was the equivalent of a high school play. The Epiphany parade and pageant involve literally hundreds of individuals in medieval costumes representing nobility, the military, and the city's major industries.

The official viewing party, sitting on the chairs on the Duomo steps, includes church officials, local dignitaries, and representatives of regional organizations. Pride of place goes to three Roman Catholic priests, all in black cassocks, with colorful hats signifying their status. Ennio Cardinal Antonelli, appointed in 2001, wears red, the bishop violet, and the monsignor black. The latter, Timothy Verdon, is an American who speaks impeccable Italian and is not only canon of the cathedral, but also an art history professor at Stanford University.

The official party watches couple after couple strolling past at a courtly pace, women in velvet gowns, men in doublets and hose. And the hats! Wide-brimmed hats, round floppy hats, hats with rolled crowns, and hats with plumes. Appreciative applause ripples from spectators standing five deep on the sidewalk. Participants form lines between the cathedral and the Baptistery, making room for the arriving drummers, trumpeters, pennant-tossers, and banner carriers in various versions of red and white, the Florentine colors.

The military wear silver helmets and crested breastplates; they carry pikes, broadswords and staffs; friars hold small wooden crosses and peasants trundle handcarts full of colored wool or clutch pitchforks and field rakes. I can't imagine the volunteer commitment required for such events, let alone the year-round costume storage that's involved. There's even a cow in a raised cage that has steps for a closer look, as if this domestic animal were some exotic beast in a zoo.

A sixty-member choir of schoolgirls, all dressed in red tunics, white stockings, and Santa hats, sing seasonal tunes ranging from *Venite Adoremus* to *Jingle Bells* while carrying out choreographed hand and arm movements. The featured soloist has a voice so sweet it makes your heart ache at the sound.

Cardinal Antonelli speaks to the children about the three magi and their relevance to Epiphany. When he asks what expensive gifts they brought for the Christ child – an easy question, since the answer has already been given that day in song and story – there is only silence from the children.

Antonelli tells them the answer, using a teacher's patient tone, then asks: "What did each of the expensive gifts symbolize?" Again, the children are silent. "Gold meant that Christ was King, incense represented his divinity, and myrrh foretold His death on the cross. But the magi also brought something else – their love," he continues. "Which do you think was the most important gift – love or expensive gifts?" This time, there is no doubt in the children's minds and they all shout: "Expensive gifts." Everyone laughs, even His Eminence.

After almost three hours of speeches and spectacle, the finale involves the firing of a cannon, rousing cheers all round, and a recorded version of Handel's *Messiah* – King of Kings, forever and ever.

The next day, gifts become less expensive as post-Christmas sales begin. Many retailers knock off 50 per cent immediately. Others start discounting at 30 per cent and work their way up to 70 per cent over the next two to three weeks. Some of the big names, particularly designers such as Armani, Ferragamo, and Zegna on classy Via de' Tornabuoni, offer no markdowns. In keeping with the end of the Christmas season, decorations are removed and the potted evergreens that have graced our streets for the last month are trucked away.

At the Sunday antiques market held in Piazza Santo Spirito, the quality of items at the fifty stalls range from good to garage sale. There's furniture and flatware, horseshoes and hand tools, table legs and tie racks, wooden hat forms and worn clothing, silver and ceramics.

At a bookstall we spot Frederick Hartt's *History of Italian Renaissance Art*. According to the stamp on the inside front cover, this copy once belonged to the library at Syracuse University. Marco, the stall vendor, is asking fifteen euros. I offer twelve. He accepts all too quickly; I should have said ten. Still, he gives us a Versace shopping bag in which to carry the 704-page tome. In the midst of January sales, designers, and dickering about a few euros, a graffiti artist has the last word. On the way home, we see this admonition written in white chalk on the wall beside the window of Escada: "Money is your excuse of beautiful."

❖

Frederick Hartt's book is a bit battered. The back cover has come unhinged, and a number of pages are loose. A rehabilitative visit to a bookbinder is required. Fortunately, this is Florence. Such a man exists only a ten-minute walk away. Shake hands with Paolo Bruscoli and you can feel every restoration job he's ever done, every new item he's ever made. His hand is powerful yet gentle, as rough as sandpaper yet somehow welcoming. He is surrounded in his shop on Via Montebello with the tools of his trade and the creations of his craft. He is not only a bookbinder but also a maker of leather goods: boxes, desk sets, albums, and briefcases. In his white smock he is a handsome, broad-chested man who stands about 190 centimeters tall, and has friendly eyes that peer over glasses perched precariously on the tip of his nose.

Paolo is the fourth generation to run the business that his great-grandfather, Egisto, founded in 1881. As he talks about the family history and the creative process, this might as well be the fifteenth century, not the modern era. Paolo is telling about his own apprenticeship as well as describing how the Medicis had an uncanny capacity to spot talent. The ruling family of patrons would pluck boys of thirteen or younger out of poverty and place them in the workshops of great artists and artisans. Not only would they learn goldsmithing or sculpting or painting, but many of them would also go on to start their own workshops. That focus on finding and training individual talent as well as transferring the techniques was a compelling reason why the Renaissance flowered in Florence for so long.

Paolo relates how, during a ten-year period that began in the 1540s, Benvenuto Cellini created *Perseus*, a monumental bronze statue of the mythological Greek hero holding the head of Medusa. The sculptor was given a house, a meal tab at a restaurant, and a bottle of wine a day – but no cash payment until the commission was complete. No bronze work of this size and complexity had ever been attempted before, so he had to experiment. Paolo's brown eyes glitter as he recounts how Cellini ordered twice as much wood as he needed in order to ensure there was enough fuel to melt the metals and shape the bronze. The overheated furnace set his house ablaze but Cellini didn't lose focus. He tossed into the inferno any and all metal he could lay his hands on, including the household pewter and cutlery. When the fire finally died down and the bronze had cooled, the statue was miraculously finished, minus three toes that were added later.

Paolo's own methods are as unique as Cellini's, but unlikely to last much longer. He is sixty-two and has no successor. His son considered joining the business but decided to go into computer programming where there was more money to be made. His daughter tried her hand and had sufficient talent, but found the life too lonely and became a bookkeeper. A nephew spent a year in the shop only to decide he wasn't suited. Paolo wishes the outcome were otherwise but he can understand. "What I like, I like for me. I showed them, but life is your own choice. Young people want to be part of something. Here, you know what you are, but you are alone. You have to trust yourself, believe in yourself."

Taking in a young apprentice from another family is no longer the option it might have once been. These days parents want their children to stay in school longer and go on to university. By the time they graduate they are too old for Paolo to teach. "In the beginning you do not enjoy gluing the whole day but you have to train your hand. You don't see the end of any-thing. At fifteen, that's okay. At eighteen or nineteen, a person can see other places [in life]. At twenty-one, they say, 'What have I done today? Nothing.'"

Watch with me while Paolo Bruscoli makes a leather-covered box. He begins by selecting the leather that he will join together with the wood in a process that will last longer than a good marriage. He can remember accompanying his grandfa-ther, Francesco, to the local tanneries to buy skins from animals raised in Tuscany. Francesco signed his name on the skins he chose to ensure he received what he'd selected. Today, most of the skins from animals raised in Italy are bought by luxury goods houses such as Gucci and Ferragamo. Paolo doesn't mind, he finds those skins too soft for what he makes. The skins he buys are top quality, but they come from South Africa and Argentina, so he can no longer pick the exact ones he wants from the pile.

After selecting the leather he makes a cedar box the size he wants, paints the inside, then spreads vegetable glue on the out-side. The glue takes a day to dry so there's plenty of time for the leather to be applied, shaped into place, and smoothed. Paolo uses calf's leather because it is supple enough for him to model yet thick enough to hold decoration. The pieces of leather, cut into strips, are laid on the box, stretched into place and flattened with a blade, then trimmed with a knife.

Once the glue is dry and the leather secure, the box is ready to be embellished and decorated with one of the eighteen hun-dred carefully numbered hand tools that are stored in glass-fronted cases. Each tool is different with intricate shapes that create designs, from a fleur-de-lys through measured rules to filigreed flourishes.

Paolo picks a wooden-handled iron from his collection, one with a metal wheel on the end that has an intertwined border motif. He heats the iron, holds the long wooden handle with both hands, and places the top of the handle against his shoulder. He presses the hot end onto a thin sliver of gold laid on the box, leans into the work to use his body weight while maintaining a constant pressure, and then rolls the wheel forward while at the same time rocking the iron slightly from side to side to ensure the full width of the design is registered. The decoration is then "beaten" onto the surface with another metal-wheeled tool and given a final cleaning. The proper combination of heat, pressure, and the master's hands, renders the gold design permanent.

Markets and products have changed since the days of Egisto and his son, Francesco, who did only bookbinding. In the third generation, Piero added leather goods, but his sales were only local. "In the time of my father, Florence was enough. In my time, I needed the world," says Paolo. Those new long-distance customers were loyal. The 1966 flood of the Arno, the river that's just a block away, severely damaged his shop. Customers from all over the globe offered money for rebuilding, but he refused. In response, some of the retailers who carried his goods doubled their usual orders and sent payment in full up front.

Photos of some of his famous clients hang on the walls and include dancer and choreographer Martha Graham, shown with the Bruscoli family. There is also a framed letter dated July 23, 2003, from Luci Baines Johnson, daughter of U.S. President Lyndon Baines Johnson along with a photo taken with Paolo in his shop. Says the letter, in part: "It reminds me of 30 years of our friendship and the treasure of your incredible talent and kindness."

Paolo enjoys making leather goods, but his favorite work is bookbinding, sewing the new backing by hand, lining the inside with silk, and embossing the leather covers. "If I make a mistake on a box, I can just throw it away. For a perfect binding, everything has to be done just right, and every book is different." In addition to producing goods for sale, Paolo has also participated in great civic projects. One of those endeavors was at Biblioteca Laurenziana, the library at the Medici Chapels. The medieval volumes could not be removed from the premises, so for eight years he and a team worked on site, repairing and restoring the leather bindings and parchment pages.

At the peak of his productive years, Paolo had five employees but the effort involved became more of a bother than it was worth. "If you have five people, your time is gone organizing. All that work, and the money in my pocket at the end of the year was the same."

Now that he is alone, he is happy and has reached a point in his career where he has full self-knowledge. "When I started out, I didn't know what level I would attain. Now I know; this is better. There is no anxiety." His only concern now is about the future for bookbinding and leather goods in general as well as for other skills that could soon be lost. "Schools now teach you how to do just a small piece of the work. I use my mind to figure out the best place for each piece of leather to go." Today's consumers prefer well-known brand names, rather than quality goods from small shops. "With Gucci you can buy something without having to know anything. With an artisan you have to know something, you have to be able to choose. You have to buy high quality for a long time to be able to recognize it."

Paolo hopes that the city will organize a program to teach young people the old ways, how to create a finished product from scratch. From such a group might come a savior willing to take over his bookbinding and leather-tooling business, but it's a long shot. More likely, his tools will end up on display in some museum. Paolo would be honored to have his life's work celebrated in such a manner, but he'd prefer continuity, as should we all. The past is more than mere memories. Without a living heritage, we are no longer as human as we once were.

❖

The problem of the disappearing artisan is more profound than the loss of one man's shop and skills. On a Saturday night at 5 p.m., about twenty people have gathered for a meeting of the Fondazione di Firenze per l'Artigianato Artistico (The Florence Foundation for Artistic Crafts). The group spends the next two hours wrestling with ways to save at least some of the local artisans who face almost certain extinction. In the last two years the foundation published three studies giving details on the history and methods involved in making leather goods, decorative paper, and clogs. The foundation also sponsored an exhibit in the San Frediano sector of Florence, a former hive of artisan activity, in the hope that such demonstrations of craftsmanship will encourage new participants.

Artists and artisans were once the backbone of Florence. In 1336, one-quarter of the city's population of one hundred and twenty thousand worked in the manufacture of wool or silk cloth and finished pieces. As the guilds grew in size and importance they formed a new social class and took an active part in running the city. Each guild had its own office, a section of the city where the *bottega* (workshops) were located, and an arbitration process to settle disputes. In the fifteenth century the fourteen most powerful and prosperous guilds commissioned sculptures of their patron saints by the likes of Donatello for display in exterior niches of Orsanmichele, a church that began life as a grain market.

By the sixteenth century there were ninety different types of specialized artisans making everything from chinaware to precision instruments. In 1765 there were two hundred and fifty thousand merchant artisans and craftsmen in Tuscany. Today in Florence, where most of the Tuscan artisans are located, that number has shrunk to six thousand, according to the Chamber of Commerce.

Six thousand sounds sizeable, but that number is deceiving. The Chamber's total includes anyone working at any firm that has eighteen or fewer employees. The description of artisan in the Chamber's census is so broad that it embraces workers who, for example, repair cars or fix household appliances. Giampiero Maracchi, a member of the foundation, puts the number of artisans in Florence at no more than two hundred. Other members claim the number is closer to nine hundred, but Giampiero is a purist. He does not think that someone who simply makes the same commercial product over and over again should be called an artisan. "In five years, that business will be gone, replaced by someone in China," he says. "How do you define artisan? It's the quality."

Giampiero was born in Florence where his family has lived for six generations. His recent ancestors were lawyers and magistrates; some of them served the Dukes of Lorraine, the nineteenth-century Austrian rulers of Tuscany. When Giampiero was sixteen his father arranged for him to work for a summer with a shoemaker so he could see that not everyone was raised in a privileged home. "I was fascinated. In some sense I was asking myself if maybe this would be a better way to spend my life than as a professional." He did not follow that path, but he did break away from the family tradition of going into law. After studying physics and agronomy in the United Kingdom, France, and the Netherlands, he became a scientist. At sixty-one, he is a climatologist and the director of the Institute of Meteorology, a national body based in Florence. Climatology may be his profession but his passion is the work of artisans and keeping those skills alive.

I am sitting with Giampiero in his apartment in southeast Florence, surrounded by a museum-quality collection of shoemaker's tools as well as displays of planes and pruning scythes. He has two sewing machines for making shoes, one in the living room and another under plastic sheeting on a balcony. Almost everything in the apartment is handmade: rugs, furniture, lamps. In a nook on the second balcony is a workshop where he indulges his passion by making clogs with wooden soles and leather uppers like those once worn by Tuscan sailors and farmers.

There are similarities between scientific research and making shoes, according to Giampiero, who believes that being an artisan is as much about headspace as handiwork. Whatever you make, you must start with a plan, gather what you need for the job, and constantly verify what you are doing before the task can be finished. "Artisans work with their brains. Their hands are just a tool for the brain. This passion I have is very useful in my job and vice versa."

The fact that the Florence Foundation for Artistic Crafts even exists at all is remarkable. The five disparate member groups that comprise the foundation include two levels of government, the Chamber of Commerce, and two trade unions, one representing the political right, the other the local left-wing elements. Florence has more Communists than most regions of Italy so the left-wing union is much larger than the more conservative right.

The foundation's next project, and perhaps the most crucial so far, is to produce a complete list of all the artisans working in Florence. Whether the total ends up to be two hundred or nine hundred, the number is down dramatically in the last fifty years. Giampiero retrieves from a nearby bookshelf *Volume I*, the Tuscan listings in a multivolume national directory published in 1958 called *Dizionario degli Artigiani d'Italia*. Declares the introduction: "How many of these artisans are there in Italy? They are a very republic in the republic; they are tens upon tens of thousands, hundreds of thousands."

Indeed, the list of artisans living in Tuscany less than fifty years ago, with photographs and descriptions of their work, runs to 642 pages. In Florence there were more than 500 leather goods companies and shoemakers, 450 tailors and dressmakers, 600 embroiderers and upholsterers, and 120 goldsmiths. Giampiero says today there are no more than half a dozen individuals who are producing quality items in those fields. In 1958, there were 112 artisans making straw hats and handbags. Now there are none. Cheap labor and Third-World production is only part of the cause. There is also a lack of appreciation by today's consumers who prefer the haughty status of logos over the high standards of the artisan. Give me Gucci over Giuseppe, they say, Ferragamo over Francesca.

Giampiero worries that the work of the foundation will fail because of community apathy. "Because the past was so big, people in Florence think we don't need to face the modern world. The past cannot come back but you can use the past to build a new era. The shoemaker used to be a laborer, a poor man who didn't earn much, and was at a low level in society. In the new version, the shoemaker can be an artist."

❖❖

The morning sun slowly burns off the fog in the valleys as our bus lumbers ever higher. We are headed for Volterra, a hilltop town in Tuscany, two hours south of Florence. If weather had

been a deterrent we would have stayed in bed. The cloud cover was so low in Florence it seemed to have settled just above our ears, but we walked to the SITA bus terminal and bought our *andata e ritorno* tickets for the round trip. After the first hour a weak sun appears, grows stronger, and slowly melts the mists to make a bedazzling day with a sky of cerulean blue.

After transferring to another bus in the village square of Colle di Val d'Elsa, the final leg of the trip is a voyage back in time across a landscape that appears not to have changed for centuries. As the road grows more winding, the scenery becomes bucolic. There are silver-leaved olive trees, orderly rows of cypress that cast long black shadows, and groves of pine that looked sculpted in the round by unknown hands. Fields come in many forms: brown plowed earth ready for planting, rumpled green corduroy with flocks of grazing sheep, and the natural suede of last year's corn stubble. Bird life abounds: finches flit from tree to tree, an unidentifiable raptor perches on a faraway wire looking for lunch, and magpies swoop about wearing their black-and-white clown suits. Among the numerous honey-stoned farmhouses only one is undergoing a major renovation. It would appear that no new construction has taken place along this road during the previous two hundred years. Framing the full panorama are four blue-gray lines of rolling hills, each closer to the horizon and less in focus than the last.

Finally, perched like a wedding cake high on a hill ahead, is Volterra, renowned for its alabaster, a form of gypsum quarried nearby that's used for carved statuary and decorative items. If there is one shop selling alabaster, there must be fifty offering a wide variety of opaque vases and lamps, lustrous serving plates and stemware, fine necklaces and brooches, as well as polished trinkets for the tourist trade.

The Etruscans were the first to work with the soft alabaster boulders, a heritage still celebrated in a workshop where an artisan casts reproductions of Etruscan statues on alabaster bases. Using copper and brass, he follows the same method as did his father who began the business fifty years ago. We listen attentively for a long time as he explains the lost wax process.

The walk west to the place where the town abruptly halts takes almost thirty minutes. The view from the cliff several hundred meters above the valley below must stretch more than twenty kilometers. In the middle distance are a series of curious erosions with gray-white sharp-peaked outcroppings that rise from the valley floor to form a miniature Alps. Centuries of rain have washed away the clay cover to create knife-sharp rivulets in the combination of limestone, sandstone, and alabaster.

Somewhere a dog barks briefly. A few pigeons coo in a backyard pen and then fall quiet. The silence that descends is like nothing I've experienced since coming to Italy. Because it continues, this heavenly hush is even better than that brief bit of peacefulness that comes in the moment immediately before sleep. The stillness is so serene I worry that my own breathing will disturb the natural balance. Think of what could be achieved amid such hushed tranquility.

In Volterra's streets, churches, and museums there is art and architecture from four eras: Etruscan stone walls and alabaster funerary urns, Roman busts and an amphitheatre with Corinthian columns, medieval carvings, and illustrated anthem books, as well as Renaissance paintings galore. Among the masterworks are two very different versions of *Christ's Descent from the Cross*. The first, in the Pinacoteca e Museo Civico, is Rosso Fiorentino's sixteenth-century Mannerist painting that shows the dead Christ's supple limbs and beatific face as he is taken down from the cross. The second, in the cathedral, consists of painted wooden figures from the thirteenth century, one of the few such creations in Italy that still has its original cross and ladder. In both places, we are the only visitors.

In the Parco Archeologico, spring is arriving. The roses have new purple leaves and the viburnum is coming into bloom. There is also the odd dandelion; in January, even a weed is welcome. At five o'clock, before we board the bus for the return trip home, we walk across the street, stand at the low wall looking west across the valley, and watch the setting sun until it is but a red speck before disappearing behind the far-off hills. The evening sky turns rosy pink and the few puffy clouds glow as if lit from within. The spectacular scene at the end of a perfect day serves as a gentle reminder. The tranquility we urban dwellers have given up for lost has not gone missing; we merely have to go looking to find it.

⊷⊷

But Italy is not all that it appears. Hidden behind the beauty there is bleakness. At 8.1 per cent, unemployment levels are among the highest in Europe. Economic growth in 2004 of

1.2 per cent was far lower than the 2 per cent average among the twelve countries that use the euro currency; in 2005 Italy was in recession. According to a survey done every five years by *The Economist* that ranks sixty countries by business environment and attractiveness to investment, Italy slipped to twenty-seventh place in 2005 from twenty-fourth in 2000. France and Germany held their previous positions, thirteenth and fourteenth respectively, while Canada, which had been ranked first, was knocked into second spot by Denmark.

At the household level, the squeeze is noticeable. One couple, both professionals, has trouble even on two salaries. "We're fine for the first three weeks but not the fourth," she says. Retailers are a bell-wether. Four years ago, at Luisa Via Roma, 70 per cent of sales were to Americans, Japanese, Canadians, and Australians. Because their currencies don't buy as many euros, today those nationals comprise only about 15 per cent of sales. But the slide has been going on for some time. At the end of the 1980s, Italy was among the most prosperous countries in the world. Today, Italy's economic performance is the worst since the Second World War.

Economic issues fade when compared with systemic problems. The very core of the country is corrupt, writes Tobias Jones in his grim book, *The Dark Heart of Italy*. "I'm beginning, finally, to understand why so much scandal, even murderous, is simply ignored in Italy," he writes. "It's too confusing to find the truth. It takes so much time. There is so much legalese and mystification that it's impossible to say what happened. The way in which that confusion and mystification occur is very simple. Italy has more laws than any other European country. The oldest university in the world, in Bologna, was founded for precisely that reason: to decipher and recipher the Justinian Codes, the *Corpus Iuris Civilis*, the *Digesto* and the points of law."

Jones, a British journalist who lived in Italy for five years and taught in Parma, loved the land but saw illegality everywhere. His book, published in 2003, asserts that many of the leading lights are dishonest: judges, politicians, even football referees. Important matches are rigged, government contracts demand kickbacks, and Prime Minister Silvio Berlusconi manipulates the media through ownership of TV networks and print outlets. "The irony is that Italy, so painfully legalistic, is as a result almost lawless. If you've got so many laws, they can do anything for you. You can twist them, rearrange them, rewrite them. Here, laws or facts are like playing cards: you simply have to reshuffle them and fan them out to suit yourself."

Berlusconi, the richest man in Italy with a fortune according to *Forbes* of US$12 billion, seems blessed with a forgiveness factor. Last month two of his closest friends received jail sentences. One, Marcello Dell'Utri, a founder of the Forza Italia party Berlusconi leads, was found guilty of aiding and abetting the Mafia and was given nine years in jail. Another friend of Berlusconi who is also his lawyer, Cesare Previti, was convicted of bribing judges in 1991 and sentenced to eleven years. So far, prosecutors have been unable to convict Berlusconi on various corruption charges.

Call me naïve, but I can do nothing about such matters. I

prefer the sunny face that Italy presents, not the dark under-belly that Jones describes. That face is unfailingly friendly, welcoming, and generous. Take an Italian couple out to dinner to thank them for something and chances are they'll bring you a gift. We got on the elevator at the Science Museum with an employee who offered to take us to the third-floor research library where she works, a place that's usually off limits to visitors. It's a beautiful room with cherry wood paneling and superb views of the Arno. Only later did we realize that we had been riding on the staff elevator. Rather than eject us, gently or otherwise, she took the opportunity to show off the space she regards as the best in the building. On another occasion, we bought last-minute tickets for *La traviata* at Teatro della Pergola, a beautiful seventeenth-century theater that's one of the oldest in Italy. Our seats were singles, in adjacent boxes, obstructed – and I mean badly obstructed – with only about one-third of the stage visible. In each box, the other three occupants were Florentines who, when they saw our respective predicaments, immediately rearranged the four moveable chairs by squeezing three into the front row and placing one behind so everyone could see. By the time the opera was over, we'd not only heard the beautiful music and seen all the staging, including the tragic ending, we'd made new friends.

Generalizations are always problematic but Italians are fun loving, genial, vivacious, and project something called *bella figura*. The words literally mean "a good figure" but the full sense of the phrase is "a good image" in the more sweeping sense of "cutting a swath" or "puttin' on the Ritz." *Bella figura* is about wanting how you look to say something about who you are.

More darkly, it could also be seen as a superficial mask under which there is too little substance. *Bella figura* describes those two Italian stallions on parade or it could also include those women on the streets who dress well and have no compunction about giving a smoldering look even before any appreciative glance comes their way.

As an outsider I can climb up on my high horse, like some famous Medici on an equestrian statue, and rail at the fakery of it but I'd rather revel in a people who always look their best and follow the adage, "Life is to be enjoyed." After all, despite my best efforts, many Italians speak much better English than I do Italian. Unlike the French who demand you speak their language, Italians don't expect fluency from foreigners. They're happy to listen to your pathetic efforts, and then they'll just as happily speak English if you'd prefer, and invite you out to dinner in their homes. To that, I can only say *grazie mille*.

❖❖

When Peter Porçal stops at the Innocenti bar on Via Nazionale at 6:45 a.m. for a cappuccino, serving staff don't need to be told that he's heading out on another of his bus-tour day trips. "They know me there. They always ask, 'Where are you going?'" It could be Venice, Lucca, Rome, or Bologna. "'You have such a wonderful life,'" he quotes them as saying, then adds, almost to himself, "Little do they know," and then he throws back his head and laughs.

Peter towers above most people in any crowd, but it is his bearing, not just his height, that sets him apart. He is handsome, with a leonine head of hair, and has one of those smiling, open faces that can charm strangers. Put him down at a rest stop on the autostrada and within seconds he will be deep into a conversation with a clutch of strangers he's just met. "Curiosity is the most important thing in life," he says. "Without it, you might as well be dead." Born of a Spanish father and a Bohemian mother, Peter received his doctorate in Art History from the Rijksuniversiteit in Utrecht, Holland. In 1970 he came to Florence at twenty-six to complete his studies and never left. Today he is the resident art historian for three schools with students in Florence: Ontario College of Art and Design, Vanderbilt, and Richmond in Florence, a program with ties to the American International University in London. He leads weekly visits by each school to local museums and churches where he delivers a three-hour lecture as he herds his "children" – as he calls them – through the Uffizi Gallery, the Bargello, or into the crypt beneath the Duomo to gawk at Brunelleschi's tomb. He also organizes regular day trips and overnight excursions by bus or train to see Byzantine mosaics in Ravenna, frescos in Arezzo, or antiquities in Rome. In the summer his uniform is a black t-shirt and blue jeans. In winter, he wears a camel coat and yellow scarf tied loosely in the haphazard Italian manner, not for warmth, but style. He always carries a green knapsack and keeps his cell phone wrapped in a plastic bag, like a lunchtime sandwich, so it is less likely to slip from his pocket and be lost.

Peter's knowledge is encyclopedic. He plays flute and piano and speaks seven languages: French, German, Italian, Spanish, Bohemian, English, and Russian. His knowledge of art is sweeping. He knows what works in which galleries have been replaced by copies, the real version secretly stashed out of sight. But he also possesses practical information such as the location of the washroom key in a pizzeria in a tiny town hours away. Most important, he makes the study of art and architecture fun by lacing his descriptions about regressive painters or the Mannerist style with anecdotes that bring the subject alive. His motto is: "Art history doesn't have to be boring."

Peter's career in Florence came about serendipitously. After he had finished his research on the frescoes by Domenico Ghirlandaio in the church of Santa Trinità he was scheduled to head back to Utrecht. As he walked near Ponte Vecchio, he spotted a sign for an apartment to rent, and impetuously decided to call. The landlord turned out to be the Italian movie star Laura Tiberti. She told him that among those who had looked at the apartment, she wanted him to be her tenant. If he called before 9 p.m. that night, the place was his.

Peter weighed the possibilities: a boring job in Utrecht or an exciting life in Florence. He phoned well before the deadline and signed the lease. Teaching positions came along with no need to look for work on his part. "You close your eyes and whatever you touch turns to gold when you are young and positive about the world."

Florence became both a home and a haven. "Whatever you look at is so old. It makes you feel safe because it has survived.

Also there is the luxury: how they live, what they sell, the restaurants they eat in. In the last thirty-five years, that's one thing that has not changed." He also enjoys the full-tilt Italian life, *feste permanente*, the permanent feast. Give a Dutchman ten euros, says Peter, and he will try to buy as many useful items as he can: five knives, five forks, and five spoons. Give an Italian ten euros and he will buy something worth fifteen euros and then worry later where the other five euros will come from. "*Fare il passo più lungo della gamba*," said Peter, which translates as "They take a step that is longer than their leg." Florence is filled with interesting people; striking up a conversation is easy. "You hit the tennis ball and they reply. Any other place they step aside and let the ball hit the wall."

Peter's first marriage ended in divorce, but after some time alone his life abruptly changed for the better with the arrival of his daughter, Chiara. He did not marry her mother, a sculptress in her early forties when their child was born. Nor do they live together; the two of them would fight too much, said Peter, but they amicably share the parenting. He picks up Chiara every day after school and spends time with her most weekends.

Peter participated in the hospital delivery and selected her names. Francesca was the first name to come to his mind, after St. Francis of Assisi. Then followed Chiara, also a saint, who was probably St. Francis's lover. The third name was Constanze, from Constanze Weber, wife of Mozart. Once Peter had chosen all three, he played around with the order to create the most poetic combination. "If you ask her her name," he said proudly, "she will say: Chiara Constanze Francesca." At seven and a half, she sings, plays violin and piano, and is likely learning art history from Peter along with the rest of us. Most of what I know about art and art history from our time in Italy, I owe to him. I'm not alone. During the last thirty years, several thousand other students who have been curious about life around them can surely say the same.

The weather has finally turned cold. In December, average daytime temperatures in Florence were a balmy 12°C to 15°C. Through most of January it's been a relatively mild 8°C to 10°C. But on January 25 there were brief snow flurries, followed by temperatures that hovered near zero for a week. *Tramontana*, the north wind, has arrived. This week, the worst of winter occurred well to the south when hundreds of motorists were stranded for two days and two nights on the highway that runs between Salerno and Reggio Calabria until they were finally rescued by the army.

By comparison, our chilly apartment is a minor annoyance. The central heating system is a German machine named Vaillant fuelled by the city gas system and contained in a small metal cabinet that hangs on the wall above the refrigerator. The box whirrs and clatters as it gamely tries to keep the apartment warm. But with one radiator per room, lofty ceilings, single-pane windows, and no insulation in the walls, it is a lost cause. Even when the system runs all day the temperature gets no higher than a brisk 19°C. We bundle up in silk long johns beneath sweaters and turtlenecks and then layer a wool fleece on top.

With or without cold temperatures, fur coats are far more prevalent on the streets of Florence than in Toronto. Mink is the most popular pelt in ladies' styles, either to the knee or full-length. Coats have a swinging cut and sculpted ends. One day during this recent chill a group of protesters stood outside La Rinascente, the nearby outlet of a national department store chain. Two among the dozen participants held a banner stretched between long sticks that declared *Vende Morte*, "sellers of death." Other members of the group blew whistles, shouted, and showed passersby posters bearing ancient photos of seal pups being clubbed. Police in two vehicles watched from a respectful distance, their engines running to keep the uni-formed occupants warm. I vainly looked for Brigitte Bardot among the rabble. With frigid temperatures and this anti-fur brigade, I could be outside Holt Renfrew on Bloor Street. I feel right at home.

❖❖

The computer screen fills with dots superimposed on a map of Tuscany: red, blue, yellow, and green. Each dot is color-coded to show where and when, in a series of two-hour periods on June 17, 2003, lightning struck during a thunderstorm that raged across the region for eight hours. This archived meteoro-logical incident is among millions of such events stored at the Laboratory for Meteorology and Environmental Modeling that's housed in a building near the Florence airport.

I have come here to learn about the sudden cold weather from climatologist Giampiero Maracchi. We'd met him as an artisan but he's also director of Istituto di Biometeorologia (Ibimet). Precipitation, ground temperature, and temperature of cloud tops, humidity, barometric pressure, wind velocity, and direction – all the phenomena that go to form weather patterns are continuously monitored using radar stations and airborne satellites. Agriculture is Giampiero's specialty so the data collected has a purpose: short-term weather forecasting for healthy crops as well as long-range predictions for improved land management. Other applied science projects under way include the monitoring of greenhouse gases as well as oil spills in the Mediterranean.

The mission of the institute is to study the impact of global warming on agricultural production. For the last fifteen years changes in the patterns of global air circulation have altered the Tuscan seasons. "Winter used to start in mid-December, now it begins in late January, but still lasts the same four-to-six weeks it always has," he says. As a result, spring arrives in mid-March, not mid-February, and that change in timing has an impact on when planting can begin in the fields or when grape vines and olive trees come alive.

Maracchi founded the Institute in the mid-1970s and has seen it grow to 150 employees, half in Florence, the rest in four other locations: Bologna, Sicily, Rome, and Naples. Facts about the weather flow from his computers: the all-time low in Florence was minus 10.6°C in 1985, the record high was 41.6°C in 1983. Days a year with temperatures above 34°C, eleven. Average rainfall, 800 millimeters. Only once every five or six years does snow fall and remain on the ground for any length of time.

In addition to his role at the Institute and its association with the National Research Council, Giampiero also teaches climatology at the University of Florence and the Italian Air Force Academy. Many of the young technicians who work under him are his former students. Just as Americans blame Canada for their cold weather, Italians hold Canada responsible for their rain. As the westerlies blow from Canada across the Atlantic they pick up moisture from the Gulf Stream and then dump rain on the cooler landmasses of Europe. If only we could figure out a way of charging for such ephemeral goods and services, such unaided exports would give new meaning to the old cliché, drawers of water.

Our conversation continues over lunch at Trattoria da Burde on Via Pistoiese, the main road linking Florence and Pistoia. The front awning is frayed and the walls need paint, but this trattoria offers traditional Tuscan cooking at its best. The three Gori brothers, Giuliano, Mario, and Fabrizio, are the fourth generation to run the place since the family became involved in 1901. Their father, Turrido, died ten years ago. Their mother, Irene, worked in the kitchen until last year when she finally retired due to failing health. She was eighty-eight.

The meal begins with a thick soup of black cabbage and corn followed by fresh pasta with meat sauce. Next comes beef tongue, boiled until tender, served in its own juice. On a separate plate are the condiments: basil and garlic sauce, pickled onions, tiny green peppers, and mayonnaise. We share a bottle of red house wine that looks about as big as the oak cask in which it was aged. Dessert is a recipe from sixteenth-century

Siena when honey was used as the sweetener. Called *cavallucci* (little horses), this warm, chewy, and oversized cookie is made with fig, orange, hazelnut, and anise accompanied by several tumblers of *vin santo*, a sweet dessert wine. Coffee *con grappa* finishes the meal and just about finishes me. Lunch, which ends at 3 p.m., has taken more than two hours. "At table," Giampiero tells me, "there is no time." I now understand the Italian need for *riposo*, an afternoon siesta. After a lunch like that, who cares a fig for the weather?

FEBRUARY

F LYING ALONG THE STREETS OF FLORENCE in a Fiat 500 feels
a bit like being a bullet at belt level. Attilio Franco, cal-
ligraphist and card maker, is driving his *cinquecento* and
demonstrating the vehicle's surprising power. "Look at this,"
he shouts as we careen wildly around a corner, "not bad for two
cylinders. It goes much faster when there is only one person in
the car." For me, this is plenty fast enough. Parked cars, trash
bins, and pedestrians are flying by my window. I reach behind
my shoulder for the seatbelt. "No seatbelt. It's a historic vehicle," he cackles as a man might when he has someone pinned
helplessly, like a butterfly on a collector's board. I'd hang on to
something if I could, but the interior of the car is so minimalist
there is nothing to grab. "It's a toy," he shouts over the roar of
the engine, and then changes gears and goes faster still.

Attilio has owned his *cinquecento* for fifteen years. Built in
1969, now in its thirty-sixth year, the car still looks brand new.
Only three meters long, and half that in width, it *is* a toy, yet

there is plenty of headroom in the front seat. The cramped back seat is a different story; it might hold two small children or one hunkered adult for the briefest of trips. The dashboard couldn't be simpler: a green light indicates the headlights are on; a red light glows when the gas is getting low. Turn the key, press a starter on the console, and that's it. Any key in the ignition will do, even one from a suitcase, all that's required is contact. Once the car is going, you can remove the key, and the rear-mounted engine will continue to run. Vespa, the stylish scooter everyone associates with Italy, has had similar longevity. First produced in 1946, Piaggio has made more than 16 million Vespas, including the current models that meet modern emission standards.

The Fiat 500 seems to take up about the same amount of space. Not for nothing is the *cinquecento* called the "sandwich" car; you can park it anywhere. According to Attilio I can buy one, fully restored, for only four thousand euros. He also owns a second car, a Mercedes, but finding parking for that larger vehicle is a problem. In Florence, a garage for such a large car would cost fifty thousand euros so he bought nine hundred square meters of land outside Florence. There, surrounded by some grass and his ten olive trees, sits his Mercedes in all its open-air splendor. When he travels long distances, he drives the Fiat to the site and does a switch.

Born in Sicily, Attilio is married and has two teenaged sons, Peter and Robert; however, he does not live with his family. After ten years of marriage, he'd had enough of Sicily's insularity but his wife wouldn't budge. He could not stay, so he left them and lives alone in Florence. Three times a year he spends a week with his family. "It takes me two or three days to adjust. The Mafia is still in control. Buildings are erected just for the profit they provide to the organization. Roads are poorly made and maintained." Economic troubles go beyond Sicily to include the entire southern part of Italy that has always been poor. For Attilio, Italy is like a centaur. The mythical being's human half represents the wealthy north; the bottom portion, the beast, is the depressed south. "It is not a democracy where there is such a difference economically. Berlusconi was elected by promising to make change, but nothing has happened."

For a time, Attilio taught English as a second language to businesspeople. At sixty-five he now lives on a small pension and supplements his income by selling his calligraphy and works on paper in a small studio near Piazza Santo Spirito. An elegant dresser, he favors velvet jackets. His face is always wreathed in a smile, his disposition relentlessly sunny. His work as a graphic artist was interrupted by a fall this month. When taking a bag of trash to the street, his foot struck the protruding metal base of a temporary sign and down he went. He put out his right hand to catch himself so hurt his wrist when he hit the pavement. An x-ray at the hospital revealed a sprain, no broken bones. They rubbed the area with an ointment for the pain, wrapped his wrist in a thick, supportive bandage, and told him he'd be fine in five days.

As injuries go, this one was relatively minor, but still, for an artist to lose the use of his working hand, even briefly, is serious. Only Attilio could perceive a benefit from the incident. "It made me realize how precious our hands are," he said. "We were given two legs, two arms, two eyes, two ears. That was not for symmetry, you know, it was for conservation."

Attilio knows better than most whereof he speaks. Stricken with polio as a boy, he uses a cane and walks with a limp. If he had full use of both legs, he might not have so easily lost his balance that night, but there it is, and he will not only live with the outcome but also learn from it.

Every time I see Attilio he's a-bubble with some bold new idea. One time he talks about becoming an agent shipping wine to wealthy Americans; the following week he announces plans to put together a string of freelance translators who will do corporate work. On another occasion he says he will be compiling a guidebook about the monuments and restaurants of Florence. He carries several calling cards, one of which says he is a consultant in psychopathology, available by appointment only.

Meanwhile, the items he makes and sells, handmade paper cards and larger display pieces, are modestly priced, from one to five euros. He also designs business cards, and buys art from artists that he re-sells to tourists. He shares the retail space with two others, so his costs are low, but the extra income is equally modest. Ah, but the view. Across the street there's a doublewide wooden doorway and a graceful Gothic arch in a fine stone building.

"I could live in a better business area," he says, "but when I look out at this medieval palace, I am enriched. The Greeks had a word for it, *kalos*. The world is beautiful. We have to adjust."

Our first encounter with Attilio was serendipitous. As we stood outside his studio he came out the door and invited us in to sit down for a chat. A few days later he introduced us to his friend Paolo Bruscoli who in turn took us to the artisanal exhibit where we met Giampiero Maracchi. That's how it goes in Florence where life is a series of chance encounters that have led us to the Società Canottieri, the rowing club where Paolo is a member.

Trophy cases and framed photographs portray members of this rowing club competing in local, national, and international races including the 1956 Olympics in Melbourne. There's a bar and dining room as well as meeting and exercise rooms. In addition to the modern workout machines, there's a deep concrete pool with fixed oars so members can sit and practice rowing in water, just like in real life.

The boat storage area looks like a large train tunnel that's maybe two hundred meters long. It has a rounded roof and is four meters across and six meters high. At one end, there's a pair of double doors that open onto a ramp leading to the Arno River; at the other end there's a workshop for repairs. All along the stonewalled sides hang members' rowing skiffs, racked four high.

On the wall near the doors to the river is a huge stone crest, a leftover from the nineteenth century when the Austrian Dukes of Lorraine ruled Tuscany and kept their horses and carriages here. Immediately above is the Uffizi Gallery where droves of tourists view art. Here, underneath, is a secret place unknown to the day-trippers.

Among the club members I meet is Franco Ciardini, who took turns with another member rowing a one-man skiff from the Arno to the Thames, Florence to London. The feat in 1987 took two-and-a-half months on a route across the Mediterranean, along a series of rivers and canals through France, across the English Channel, then up the Thames River.

The club began in 1911 in a wooden structure on stilts with a verandah near the Santa Trinità Bridge, where members shared the river with women who washed clothes on stone steps. In 1933, a Florentine-born member of Benito Mussolini's staff decided the club deserved better quarters, so he arranged for the members to become tenants in this special space with the Italian government as landlord. Every so often the director of the Uffizi makes noises about evicting the club and taking over the space, but so far nothing has happened.

Bookbinder Paolo Bruscoli's skiff, the *Bruscolo*, hangs near the double doors to the river. His father, Piero, was a rower and a member of a four-man team that won a national championship. Piero gave Paolo this skiff in 1960 when he was eighteen and all his friends were getting scooters. Three times a week Paolo takes down the skiff, carries it over his head to the river, and rows ten thousand meters during the next hour. "You get in your boat and it clears your mind," says Paolo. "You are in the heart of Florence, but the noise rises, so there is a peacefulness on the river."

The English terms *skiff* and *sculler* are used by the Italian-speaking members because, as they point out, the sport originated in England where world-famous races are held at

Henley and Hammersmith. Paolo's skiff is six meters long, weighs seventeen kilograms and is made of Honduran cedar. There's an open cockpit where he sits on a sliding seat, a metal apparatus to hold the oars, and fixed-position shoes. Most of the skiffs at Canottieri are like Paolo's, built for one person, although there are a few two-seaters as well as a large Venetian gondola that requires four rowers.

Evening dining outside on the riverbank is a particular pleasure. The site is so close to the Ponte Vecchio that you can sit and watch the sun set underneath the bridge. The only nuisance is the nutria, a furry rodent that's a cousin to the beaver but has a scaly tail. Nutria live in burrows, swim in the river, and forage on the grassy banks. Each generation becomes bolder about begging for food. A couple of years ago their scrounging got to the point where, if diners at the rowing club did not throw scraps, some of the animals would paw at a human leg to gain attention. The club decided to have the animals trapped and taken away. They expected four or five but caught twenty-seven. Conditions have improved but even now the animals have reappeared on the river in growing numbers. Offspring of their offspring will soon be back at table, begging.

When an artist sells a painting, she rarely sees the work again. The buyer takes the framed canvas home, hangs it, and the image disappears from public view. For Irma Schwegler, the creative experience is far different. She is a seamstress and a tailor so her clients regularly wear her work when they visit her shop. "I'm always happy when I see my clients walking on the street because they are happy to wear my clothing," she says.

As if on cue, Sandra Guerrarri shows up at Irma's shop, Old Fashion Sartoria, on Via Gran Bretagna. Sandra is wearing a wool outfit made with what's known as Casentino cloth, boiled wool in burnt orange with green lining and a green dress to match. The two vibrant colors are traditional in the Casentino, the nearby valley of the Upper Arno.

Old Fashion Sartoria is a celebration of the past. As with that client's outfit, many of Irma's patterns and textiles are based on Tuscan country wear of forty years ago. A gentleman's corduroy hunting jacket comes with deep open-topped pockets large enough to hold game birds shot in the field. In keeping with modern times, there is also a smaller inside pocket for a cell phone. Prices start at 90 euros for a sleeveless vest of *fustagno* (a velvet-like material), rise to 750 euros for a handmade jacket, and go as high as 1,200 euros for a made-to-measure three-piece wool suit. In the summer, Irma also carries a line of linen outfits and cotton skirts, all made using natural dyes.

Born in Lucerne, Switzerland, Irma, forty-one, has been sewing for twenty years. She attended a special school for three years, splitting her time each week between the sewing classes and a dressmaker's shop where she studied design, fabrics, sewing methods, and how to market to clients. Before opening her own shop, she spent a further two years working as an apprentice with a men's tailor in Florence. Compared to German or Swiss clothing where the style is square, with the shoulders heavily padded, a smoother, more modeled look is preferred in Italy. "Men's clothing is much more complicated and Italian men are very difficult. If he sees himself in the mirror, he will notice if the sleeve is two millimeters too long. My work must be perfect."

Her small store was formerly a butcher's shop. In the front room finished items are displayed – vests, jackets, skirts, hats, and capes – as well as clogs fashioned after those formerly worn by fishermen. This slip-on footwear, handmade in Lucca, has wooden soles, calf-leather uppers, and an open toe so the water and sand that collect can more easily wash away.

Hand-painted shelves hold an extensive library of books from which Irma draws her ideas for designs. A hallway leads past a dressing room on the left, formerly the cold room for meat, then on to her workroom at the rear. Excellent light comes from three fluorescent fixtures and a pair of glass doors giving onto a small garden of lavender and dusty miller. There are three sewing machines, a large worktable, ironing board, industrial-sized presser, and a row of paper patterns hanging on a long pole representing all of her customers. "When you're working alone, you have to be very organized. I need to work quickly."

Even so, a suit requires forty-five hours of her time and two fittings during the six weeks that elapse from the selection of style and material to the finished product. In her own way, Irma is following in the footsteps of the nineteenth-century Arts and Crafts movement in Britain represented by William Morris, or Bauhaus in twentieth-century Germany, where no differentiation was seen between art and craft. "Art is not only painting and sculpture but also clothing if they are pieces made specifically for you with a special textile," Irma says. "What once was craft has become art." In such a world, the customer also has a duty. "People don't only have to be able to pay but they have to understand, too."

❖

On a Friday morning we wend our way to the train station in Florence even though our planned weekend in Rome may have been marred by a strike. On Tuesday, transport workers announced a work stoppage beginning at 9 p.m. Thursday that's scheduled to last twenty-four hours as a protest about unsafe working conditions. The government proposed an eight-hour strike on Friday from 9 a.m. to 5 p.m.

On Wednesday, with the two sides still negotiating and no news about the outcome, Peter Porçal has found a ticket seller at the station who claims inside knowledge. Whatever the outcome of the talks, the wicket wizard says that two Eurostar trains will leave Florence on schedule Friday morning for Rome. We buy our advance tickets and cross our fingers.

The wizard was right. Despite the strike our train departs and arrives on time. The wacky experience where strike and regular routine can co-exist brings to mind a joke the Italians like to tell that mocks the Swiss and their infamous attention to precision and punctuality. Christ arrives in a village and sees a woman in the streets who is tearing out her hair and weeping. "I am in anguish," she tells the Saviour. "My husband has just died and I don't know what I'll do without him." "Take me to him," says Christ, who raises her husband from the dead. In the next village, there is a similar tragic scene. Christ asks, "What is the matter, my daughter?" "My husband is dead and life is no longer worth living." Christ goes to this woman's house, repeats the miracle, and brings her husband back to life. In the third village Christ comes upon a man, crying. "What troubles you, my son, why are you in such despair?" "I am Swiss," he replies, whereupon Christ stands with him and they weep together.

On the first day in Rome we tromp twelve kilometers to see some of the city's most famous tourist spots: the Pantheon, Trevi Fountain, the Colosseum, the Spanish Steps, St. Peter's, and the Sistine Chapel in the Vatican, recently restored to the original vibrant colors.

By night we walk past the Roman ruins of Augustus and Trajan, the latter with its thirty-meter column with spiraling reliefs that portray his military campaigns. Nearby is the spectacular floodlit sight of a building so big that it has four names. Built in the nineteenth century, this mammoth white marble edifice with a long flight of steps is Il Vittoriano or the Altar of the Nation, but it's also called the Wedding Cake and the Typewriter because of the semi-circular row of columns that are fifteen meters high and look like the arms on the keys of a typewriter. On top two huge chariots with horses represent Italian liberty and unity; in front – the world's largest equestrian statue – stands a ten-meter bronze of Victor Emmanuel II, Italy's first king.

While on foot, regular sustenance is important. It's hard to find a bad espresso or cappuccino in Italy. Any bus station serves excellent versions but the best coffee in the country must be at Rome's Sant'Eustachio il Caffè where the espresso is creamy sweet on the tongue and as thick as a milkshake. In Florence, Perchè No? had won our vote for best gelato, but it's beaten by Rome's Gelateria Giolitti on Via degli Uffici del Vicario. Fifty flavors of ice cream, all fresh. We try four of them: Grand Marnier, pistachio, black cherry, and lemon. *Magnifico*.

Visitors rightly rave about the handsome young men who make up the Swiss Guards at the Vatican in their distinctive Renaissance uniforms with blue-and-yellow stripes, but after seeing a dozen medieval street parades in Florence, the Swiss Guards look a little ho-hum. Less well known, but more impressive, are the guards at the Quirinal Palace. Once the summer home of popes, then the royal residence, the Quirinal Palace has been the dwelling of the president of Italy since after the Second World War when citizens voted to end the monarchy and create the modern republic.

The president is protected by 180 men, each of whom must be at least 195 centimeters tall – that's almost 6 feet 5 inches – to serve. Add a helmet that's topped by some fearsome coiled animal plus a plume as big as a horse's mane and they cannot help but command respect. The rest of the uniform is equally impressive. On ceremonial occasions the cavalry wear red jackets and brass breastplates, but even for daily guard duty the jackets are dark blue with brass buttons, red piping, and white stand-up collars. There are medals on the left breast, crests on the sleeves, white gloves, a sword with dangling white tassels, light blue pants with a dark blue stripe, black leather boots that rise above the knee, and silver spurs. We speak with one of the guards who four years ago met a Toronto policeman who was holidaying in Rome. The guard visited his new acquaintance the following year. In conversation this guard was a gentle giant.

History, art, and architecture may be what draw you to the Eternal City, but the streetscapes are the biggest surprise. Come round any corner and there could be a flower market such as the one in Campo dei Fiori where vendors have been selling apple blossoms and branches bearing ripe lemons for five hundred years. Another street offers a seventeenth-century Baroque church, San Carlino alle Quattro Fontane (St. Charles at the Four Fountains), with its white-on-white oval interior designed by Francesco Borromini. He created his own architectural language by bending and twisting elements in ways that foreshadowed modern structures such as the Guggenheim in New York. Or you might come upon Santa Maria sopra Minerva, the city's only Gothic church, beside the Dominican convent where Galileo stood trial in 1633 for his heretical belief that the universe revolved around the sun. Saint Catherine is buried beneath the main altar. Well, her body is here, but her head is in Siena, a division worthy of Solomon. You hardly need a map to amble from Roman ruins to Raphael's frescoes and then on to one of the finest open spaces in the world, Piazza del Popolo.

In the center of this oval plaza is the three-thousand-year-old obelisk of Pharaoh Ramses II that was carried back as booty from Egypt by Emperor Augustus. At one time, there were thirty-nine such obelisks in Rome. Today, there are thirteen. For centuries, there was a widespread belief that the carved hieroglyphics represented the wisdom of the ancient Egyptian culture. In fact, once translated, the inscriptions turned out to be bureaucratic announcements about administrative matters. Surrounding the obelisk is a fountain with four Egyptian lions, water spewing from their mouths, and a few graceful steps where we sit for two hours, Sandy with her sketchbook, enjoying the pageantry of local life.

Road traffic has been relegated to the far periphery of the stone-paved piazza that must measure four hundred meters across and is the largest public space in Italy. Except for the sound of some children riding the stone lions, this is about as quiet as Rome can get. On the east side of the piazza is a four-tiered Roman terrace with statues of Neptune and the Four Seasons, Corinthian columns, and a lookout. On the north side, an arched gate built in the sixteenth century, the west side is open, and on the south sits a pair of small churches, each the twin of the other, giving an unusual sense of symmetry.

It is mid-February but the temperature feels like 15°C in full sun. Teenage girls in low-cut jeans bare their bellies and the cracks of their bums. Teenage boys ogle this new version of cleavage. Someone dressed in a Spandex black-and-gold outfit with a Pharaoh's mask bows from the waist whenever a passerby drops a clanking coin into his metal pail. A man opens a wooden box at the fountain and lets loose three pet magpies on long leashes of fine chain. After they have splashed about

and sipped the water, one bird sits on his master's shoulder while another, on command, perches on his chest and kisses his lips. The third bird pecks unhappily at his restraint.

Every few minutes there are new arrivals. Thirty bicyclists appear, confer briefly, and then silently roll away. Next come five men on horseback, looking like refugees from a spaghetti Western, the hooves of one of the horses slipping dangerously on the pavement. A man plays a hurdy-gurdy to raise money for an operation to fix his badly disfigured face.

In three days we have viewed St. Peter's bones, Pope John XXIII's mummified body, and much unforgettable art and architecture, but the most memorable moment was a scene we chanced upon in Sant'Ignatio. The church was packed with pilgrims practicing *gruppi di preghiera*, a form of primal therapy group prayer that involves the laying on of hands. Individuals with various maladies and afflictions are accompanied by friends and family. After some personal witnessing, and a sermon by an Italian-speaking American priest, each group stands and holds their outstretched hands over their seated friend or family member. The energy field is palpable, a demonstration of the democratization of the modern-day church. No longer does the hierarchy rule, ordinary people with faith have personal power. The incident is so moving it brings tears even to the eyes of a tight-assed Presbyterian like myself. On this weekend, Rome has been equally potent, laying her healing hands on us.

❖

Because we expressed an interest, our leather craftsman friend, Paulo Bruscoli, has invited Sandy and I to watch while he operates his *bilanciere*, or fly press, a formidable piece of machinery in his two-level basement where there are eight different work areas crammed with equipment, including three *bilancieri*, several presses for book binding, various paper cutters, work tables, and metal shelves that hold leather skins and paper supplies.

Paolo's assignment is to make two hundred copies of a 15 x 15 cm plaque for the Associazione Antiquari d'Italia. This is a repeat order so new members of the antique association can place the designation in their store windows. The square leather plaque has beveled edges and bears the emblem of the group: a blue bust of Dante surrounded by a circular version of the group's name in gold lettering. The end result looks simple, but the creation of each plaque involves a dozen steps – all done by hand.

Before we arrived Paolo had made the individual wooden forms with beveled edges, cut each piece of leather to size, dampened the leather to make it more malleable, folded the corners neatly, and glued the leather in place. Once each piece had dried, he polished the leather using a heated burnisher, a rounded metal utensil, to create a lustrous, shiny finish.

The pieces are now ready for application of the two-color design. The fly press, made of cast iron by Karl Krause of Leipzig sometime between the First and Second World Wars, is about Paolo's height and has two flat plates, an upper and a lower, at chest level. The upper plate is heated using a built-in furnace that's fired by a gas line from the city system. To the underside of the upper plate Paolo attaches a stamping device in bronze with the letters spelling out the name of the association. While the metal letters heat to between 90°C and 120°C, he makes a four-sided cardboard form and tapes it onto the bottom plate to hold and position the leather plaque.

Once everything is ready, he pulls over a cart with a stack of leather-covered plaques along with squares of thin gold and blue papers that will supply the color for transfer. The first plaque is placed on the lower plate, a piece of gold film is laid on top of the plaque, the plate is slid into place, and then the upper plate is drawn down using a long wooden arm. Pressure is applied for a few seconds to squeeze the plates together, the arm is returned to its upright position, and *bravo*, the words have been permanently heat imprinted on the leather. Close inspection reveals the stamped motif is slightly out of kilter; adjustments are made, and there's another trial run.

How does Paolo know how much pressure to apply? The answer to the question comes not in words, but in a noise made in the throat that sounds like "ayyyh," a musical note that starts high and ends lower, accompanied by a hand gesture with the thumb and first two fingers forming a circle as much to say, "After forty years, I just know from the feel."

He finds the right feel and creates several dozen plaques with the gold lettering in the proper position. The second stamping, the blue Dante, will be more difficult because the temperature range for blue is narrower than the gold. He removes the metal letter form with a pair of tongs, attaches the Dante form to the upper plate, and waits for it to heat. After a few minutes he pulls the arm, but the register is off and Dante is not precisely in the center. After some adjustments, Paolo finds the right combination of temperature and pressure. Most people wouldn't be bothered by slight irregularities but the level of excellence Paolo demands of himself is what keeps him going. Once the two hundred are complete he will attach a hinge, covered in silk moray, so they can stand in the shop window.

While he produces plaques, Paolo talks about visiting this basement as a boy, sitting on a stool and watching in silence for hours while his father and grandfather worked with these same machines. They had it lucky – their sons wanted to go into the business, so the two previous generations had a place to go to as long as they wanted. In later life, Paolo's grandfather, Francesco, loved to work with large books despite a heart condition that made such heavy work difficult. He'd need help, but help was always at hand because his son, Piero, was there.

For a break, Paolo helps Sandy create embossed paper. She has brought along a design she drew, a rectangular form with two straight sides and two that curve. One of the four corners will actually disappear off the edge of the paper. With a knife blade he makes a negative and a positive of the design from cardboard, in effect a frame to hold the rectangular shape and a copy of the shape itself. Then he glues the cardboard rectangle onto the upper plate of another fly press and tapes the frame to the bottom plate. He puts a piece of artist's paper between the two plates. For paper stamping, no heat is required, just pressure.

Sandy has watched Paolo work the sliding bottom plate and wooden arm long enough this morning so that she knows the procedure and is able to create, in the first pass, a finished version with her design reproduced as a dented impression in the paper. Paolo returns to his leather plaques and lets her make her own paper, complete with embossed design. "I love the rhythm of this work. It's very soothing," says Sandy. "I could do this all day." The embossed paper will be used for pencil sketches, perhaps watercolor paintings as well. After a few minutes, Sandy has created thirty such individual pieces, all looking very professional. If only she were fifteen again, maybe Paolo would have found his apprentice and successor.

❖

The visit begins with wine. The Caffè Fiaschetteria Italiana offers six different Brunello wines by the glass, ranging from the four-star 1998 at six euros a glass to the very best of the most recent vintage years, the 1995 and 1997 five-star Riservas, at thirteen euros for a glass. This caffè is in Montalcino, a walled medieval hilltop town 120 kilometers south of Florence, a region famous for the robust red wine known as Brunello di Montalcino.

The caffè, opened in 1888, was owned by Ferruccio Biondi-Santi who is credited with inventing Brunello di Montalcino after identifying a distinctive sub-species of the Sangiovese grape in his vineyard. He called the grape Brunello because of its dark skin, since *bruno* is Italian for dark. The food in the caffè is unremarkable but the extensive wine list and Liberty architecture style are more than enough to make the stop worth-while. The interior features glass-fronted cases, mirrored walls, red velvet banquettes, yellow marble tabletops, and ceramic floor tiles with floral motifs.

We are in Montalcino this weekend to attend *Benvenuto Brunello* (Welcome Brunello), an annual celebration when local producers offer the first tastings of vintages now ready for sale. Part of the reason for the success of Brunello is the stringent set of rules under which wine is produced. The robust wine released each year comes from the harvest four years earlier – five years in the case of the Riserva – on this occasion the 2000 Brunello and the 1999 Riserva are being introduced.

Think of the global flutter over Beaujolais Nouveau every November when that raw young French wine appears on restaurant tables. Multiply that hullabaloo into a gathering of 150 local producers all offering free samples of vintage wine to thousands of knowledgeable tasters from the trade and you get some idea of the clamor generated by this four-day weekend.

On Friday and Saturday more than one hundred interna-tional wine writers and journalists gather in the medieval fortress that dominates the village. The experts sit at tables while sommeliers bring them wines for tasting. Such a display by oenologists is a little out of my league, but thanks to Marie Parrocel-Pirelli, owner of Millesimi, the shop in Florence where we buy our wine, we have invitations to the Sunday and Monday exhibits when members of the trade first taste the new offerings.

With the show due to open in the Fortessa at two o'clock Sunday and then re-open Monday at 10 a.m., we visit Caffè Fiaschetteria Italiana for a warm-up tasting from previous years and to learn a little history. After all, the story of Brunello di Montalcino is not just about a quality product, it is also about the power of marketing, and why it is that some wines become more world-famous than others.

Part of the reason has to do with image. At one time Bordeaux wines were the engine that pulled other French wines along, particularly with Americans, but lately the top Bordeaux wines have been unable to help mediocre offerings from other vintners. As a result, many of the small producers are struggling to survive. In addition to changing tastes, political and social issues have also played a role. "Italy is now No. 1 in wine exports to America, and its popularity owes a great deal to the country's positive image with Americans," James Suckling, Italy-based European bureau chief of *Wine Spectator* wrote in the December 15, 2004, issue. "To many consumers, Italian wines represent more than what's in the bottle; they evoke a lifestyle and benefit from a love for all that's Italian. Our parents drank Bordeaux, went to Paris on holiday, and wore Hermès clothes, but our generation drinks Italian wines, vacations in Florence, and wears Armani."

But before any good wine can be poured there must be the correct pairing of climate and soil. Montalcino is about seven hundred meters above sea level and sits on the divide between the cool continental conditions of northern Tuscany and the southern warmth of the Mediterranean. The sun-drenched slopes and cool temperatures at night, in combination with a particular grape, the sangiovese, produces ruby red Brunello. Brunello was just another little-known wine until 1978 when two American brothers, John and Harry Mariani, arrived in Montalcino. They had made their fortune with Riunite, for more than thirty years the best-selling Italian wine in the United States.

Locals were outraged when the brothers leveled some local hills as they created the estate of Castello Banfi, but when their wines began arriving in 1982 the Marianis began to win respect. Banfi's global outlook and modern marketing methods changed Brunello forever. In 2004, Banfi was named Italy's best winery for the eleventh consecutive year. Before the Banfi revolution, there were only a few dozen producers of Brunello. Now there are two hundred.

But the Marianis also had a solid base on which to build. In 1967 twenty-two local producers set aside petty rivalries and banded together to form Consorzio del Vino Brunello di Montalcino. The consortium gained further legitimacy in 1970 when Brunello became the first wine appellation in Italy to be granted official recognition with the coveted DOCG, *denominazione di origine controllata e garantita*, indicating stringent rules are involved.

Mario Ciacci, seventy-five, was among those founding fathers. "This wine is aged five years so time is very important. This wine is a good expression of the land, full-bodied and filled with tannins," says Ciacci whose vineyards, Abbadia Ardenga, produce ten thousand bottles a year. "The wine is my

life. I love the tradition. I try to put inside the wine all the tradition of twenty, thirty, forty years ago."

In addition to tradition, there are stringent guidelines that
producers must follow if they want to use the Brunello name.
"Everyone has to follow the rules," Ciacci tells me, adding with
a laugh, "almost like Russia." Rules include production using
only grapes from the region (nothing trucked in), a minimum
number of hectares under cultivation, no chemical additives, at
least two years aging in oak barrels (many producers leave the
wine more than three years) and another six months in the
bottle. Some connoisseurs will wait up to twenty years before
drinking Brunello.

The 1999 Riserva released this weekend was declared to be
better than the widely praised 1997 vintage. The 2000 was less
well received. Those privileged few who have already had
sneak previews of the 2001 wines say they are much better than
2000, whereas the 2002 and 2003 vintages both suffered because
of weather. In 2002 there was too much rain; 2003 had too little.
Worse, the daytime and night temperatures during both years
were too similar, thirty-six degrees during the day and thirty-
two at night. The year 2004 was also hot during the day, but
nighttime temperatures fell to twenty degrees, a more beneficial
range for proper growth of the grapes.

Brunello is too expensive to appear on every table. An excellent bottle of 1995 Riserva sells for seventy-five U.S. dollars in
North America. Total production of Brunello is just a spit in the
global bucket, about five hundred thousand cases a year. But
the experts place Brunello among the best in the world and can

become carried away on poetic wings when writing about it. "At its best, there is a sweetness of fruit in Brunello coupled with firm but smooth tannins, aromas suggestive of roasted chestnuts and plum confiture, a spicy component reminiscent of the local panforte cake, hints of the scent of iris and, most significantly, an unmistakable earthy component that one associates with briar and tobacco, anise and roasted coffee," wrote Edward Beltrami in a cover story on Brunello in the October/November 2000 issue of *The Wine News*.

Many producers of Brunello di Montalcino are family businesses. At nineteen, Tommaso Cortonesi represents the fifth generation at La Mannella. Of their sixty hectares of land, ten hectares (twenty-five acres) are in vineyards that produce twenty-four thousand bottles annually of Brunello di Montalcino, Grappa di Brunello, and Rosso di Montalcino, a younger and less expensive line. Olive trees occupy three hectares with the rest of the land in fields and forest. The land is stony, a welcome attribute for growing grapes. Rocks soak up the sun during the day and radiate warmth into the surrounding soil all night.

With his father Marco watching proudly, Tommaso swirls a small amount of the family's Brunello in my tasting glass, dumps the wine into a nearby canister, and then pours more wine into my glass. That initial swirl, he explains, prepares the glass to best embrace the wine's aroma. I put my nose in the glass as he describes the fruity bouquet, pointing out in particular the *lamponi*, or raspberries. I take a sip. Even such a small amount feels velvety rich on the tongue and then explodes in my mouth with hints of fruit and vanilla, or so it seems to me. I can spit out the wine, or I can swallow, the choice is mine. I swallow. Waste not, want not. It may only be mid-morning here but the sun is over the yardarm somewhere. The taste lingers in my mouth; that's what they call a long finish.

These days, parents and grandparents who pass along pruning techniques are not enough. Increasingly, vintners are hiring experts in taste and technology. Another vintner, Piero Palmucci of Poggio di Sotto, for example, employs Giulio Gambelli, who holds the industry designation *Maestro Assaggiatore*, Master Taster. Lucio Brancadoro, a professor of agriculture at the University of Milan, advises Palmucci on the density of plantings and other equally arcane matters. "I don't say I'm number one, it's very personal," says Palmucci. "My wine, you can like it or not, is a traditional and natural production. It's my work but this is the kind of business you must do with love."

Tough love is part of the process in his twelve hectares of vineyards on sloping land that rises above Sant'Antimo, a twelfth-century Benedictine abbey near Montalcino. To ensure top quality from Poggio di Sotto, Palmucci thins the vines and throws away those grapes at the end of July so the remaining fruit can absorb all available nourishment. At harvest, five workers do nothing but cull more of the unwanted grapes. In all, he discards half of the grapes that grow on his vines. "The 2000 is not as thick as the 1995, but it's very pleasant, smoother, and easier to drink. The 1995 can wait another five years, the 2000 is ready to drink now," he says.

Moving from table to table to taste the different wines is not a simple process. The aisles are jammed only two hours after the doors open and stay that way all day. Most of the attendees are male, the average age about forty. Sprinkled throughout the throng are some bespoke suits with hand-sewn lapels. More typical is a man in a cashmere sweater with a scarf folded in half with one end threaded through the loop created. His hair is silvery, combed back and curly, and there's a cell phone glued to his ear as he swirls the contents of his glass. He sniffs the bouquet, takes a sip, closes his eyes, spits the wine into a nearby container, chews a cracker, and then moves on to the next vintner. Conversations among Italians are always exuberant, even about mundane matters like the weather, so wine chatter is high on the Richter scale of animation.

Once you spy a producer who is not occupied with another taster, and you scoot into position with empty glass proffered, a certain ritual must be performed. No producer wants any residue of a competitor's wine to affect the taste of his Brunello. Paper towel or cloth cannot be used to wipe out your glass because the aroma might be altered. Vincenzo Abbruzzese, of Valdicava, uses bottled water to rinse my glass, and then pours, swirls, and dumps out some of his wine. Only then is the glass ready to hold his 1999 Riserva, Madonna del Piano. "You may have had a wonderful wine in your glass, but I want to show you my *terroir*," he says, using the French word that describes how the wine takes on the specific characteristics of the grapes, microclimate, soil, and history. "I want you to start with a new aroma." Even to a flannel-mouthed novice like myself, this is by far the best wine I have tasted all day. (The authoritative *Wine*

Spectator agrees. In the publication's May 15, 2005, edition the 1999 Madonna del Piano is given 96 on a scale of 100. "Fantastic aromas of ripe fruit and coffee, with hints of plum and cedar," says the review. "Full-bodied, with lovely, velvety tannins and a long juicy finish. Big and glorious. The greatest wine ever from here.") Only fifteen hundred cases were made; retail price is US$128 per bottle.

Abbruzzese's grandfather planted the first vines at Valdicava but his son became a banker in Siena so the family business skipped a generation. Vincenzo began working with his grandfather twenty years ago. "The most important characteristic is not the power, but the velvet, the balance, and the harmony," he explains. To achieve all that, Abbruzzese employs a winemaker, Attilio Pagli, and an agronomist, Andrea Paoletti. In wine, the big names move around like sports superstars. Paoletti used to be with Antinori, one of the major producers of Chianti Classico.

Abbruzzese knows that wines don't sell themselves, no matter how good they are, so he actively markets his product. In November 2004, he was one of forty producers of Brunello who visited Toronto and New York to hold one-day group tastings for the trade in each city. He regularly participates in events sponsored by retailers. In April 2004, for example, he and his wines were featured at a tasting and dinner sponsored by Wine Cellars of Annapolis, Maryland. "A great wine is born in the vineyard, second in the cellar," he said. "In the cellar, our technology is the best. Now, we have to understand the soul of the property."

I'll never be an expert on wine. One weekend couldn't possibly be enough to give me more than a glimpse into the complex world of winemaking. Compared to agribusiness in Canada, where some crops are grown on hundreds of acres, the amount of land needed for wine is minuscule. You could walk the entire boundary of a typical ten-hectare Brunello vineyard in fifteen minutes.

But you don't. You stop, you prune, you peer, you pick, and you patiently wait. Along the way, you learn. But even then, there's always more to discover. Think about Vincenzo Abbruzzese, a gracious man in a gray suit, saying that he still needs to understand the soul of his property. Imagine. The Abbruzzese family has produced wine on this same *terroir* for decades and there remain mysteries yet to be solved. No, a weekend is not nearly enough time. And neither is a hundred years.

MARCH

TURN THE CORNER AT THE ACCADEMIA DI BELLE ARTI and there he is, at the end of a long hallway: *David*. Of all the artwork in all the world, Michelangelo's *David* is the first piece that literally takes my breath away. I gasped when I saw him. Part of the reason is his sheer size. At four meters tall, standing atop a two-meter-high plinth, the closer you get the bigger he becomes.

But *David's* monumental size isn't the only reason for reverence. His sheer physical beauty is something to behold. Set in his own domed space, *David* is at once familiar and foreign: familiar because his physique has become an international icon, foreign because in person there is so much else to see. There are the too-large hands, the too-small penis, the delicate curls, and the impossible pose. He is looking left and leaning right, his weight on the toes of one foot, the other foot planted behind, one shoulder low, the opposite hip high, and the left hand poised off the shoulder holding a sling. Try to hold that position for sixty seconds and see how uncomfortable it becomes.

Unlike some other equally famous works, viewers treat Michelangelo's *David* with respect. In the Louvre, for example, tourists use forbidden flash to photograph the bemused smile of *Mona Lisa* despite constant shouted reminders in four languages by museum staff. *David* seems to inspire contemplative silence among his more than 1 million annual visitors.

Robert Morris, one of the five artists asked to commemorate with their art *David's* five hundredth anniversary in 2004, created a video called *The Birthday Boy* that's showing in a nearby room. The two-part video features a pair of art professors, a man and a woman, speaking at a lectern in front of *David* who constantly morphs from the nude statue through various forms including a *David* wearing camouflage pants, a black nude female, a Mona Lisa with a moustache, and finally, the artist himself, nude. "We all need heroes. And the heroic. Grandeur demands the heroic," goes the speech that's riddled with irony. "And, of course, we can't get by without our enemies because without enemies we could not invent heroes. So let's hear it for Michelangelo. He knew two things. One, that the young and sexy hero lasts longest if he can be freeze-dried into art. And two, only the awe and spectacle of the monumental will do the job."

Michelangelo's *David* was originally meant to be shown high above the street, but when he was unveiled in 1504 everyone immediately agreed that the magnificent statue deserved more prominence closer to eye level. The statue stood in the piazza in front of Palazzo Vecchio until 1873 when it was moved inside to the Accademia to preserve it from further deterioration caused by the elements.

David solidified Michelangelo's reputation and he went on to enjoy financial success. The members of the Della Robbia family could be called the first capitalist artists. They had molds they used for their ceramic plaques. You could go into their workshop and order 150 Annunciations, all to look the same, and come back in six months to pick them up.

But if money earned was a measure, Michelangelo was by far the most successful artist, not just of the Renaissance but of all time. A recent book by Rab Hatfield, *The Wealth of Michelangelo*, estimates the artist's fortune at his death was fifty thousand florins or about US$65 million in today's dollars. At one point, Pope Clement VII paid him a salary that was the equivalent of US$600,000 a year. Yet despite his wealth, Michelangelo dressed like a bum, rarely washed, and was always worried where his next meal would come from. Even in death, he was different. Michelangelo's burial in Florence did not take place until one month after he died, but despite the passage of time his skin was still soft and he smelled like roses. If the tale isn't true, it was well invented, as the Italians would say. As was his wish, his tomb is just inside the main door of Santa Croce so that on Judgment Day the first thing he sees out the door will be the Duomo.

Michelangelo's *David* has been attacked and damaged on three occasions, most recently in 1991 by an Italian painter who took a hammer to a toe on the Biblical hero's left foot before he could be restrained. But of all the assaults, none has been more controversial than the cleaning just completed in 2004. Most art restoration is conducted out of sight with little public attention.

But when noted works such as the Sistine Chapel or *David* are involved, experts offer vastly differing opinions and media hype ensues.

The first person retained to clean the marble was Agnese Parronchi, who dresses like a cowboy, smokes incessantly, and had previously cleaned other works by Michelangelo. Hired in 2002, Parronchi proposed using only dry materials, small brushes, and chamois cloths, a method she regarded as the least invasive, but the authorities at the Accademia insisted she work with wet poultices containing chemicals. She refused, saying that the proposed solvents were too harsh, and resigned the commission. Her principled stance split the art community. Some saw her as a pariah but thirty-nine Renaissance scholars proposed further independent study before work began.

The Accademia listened to no one and immediately hired Venetian restorer Cinzia Parnigoni who happily did their bidding. The official description claims Parnigoni used distilled water applied to the marble surface using compresses of cellulose pulp and meerschaum placed on sheets of rice paper. Peter Porçal, who visited *David* during the nine-month cleaning, is dubious about the benign depiction. "It was chemistry," he said. "You could smell it." Peter had a happy personal experience with the thorough work of Parronchi, who had resigned the commission. He took a wooden crucifix to her for restoration and when she finally phoned to tell him it was ready – fifteen years later – so much time had passed that he could no longer remember how big the work was. "I'll bring it home by taxi," he told her. "Oh no, you can carry it on your bike," she said. Parronchi joked that she should pay Peter for keeping the cross so long. After all that time, she charged no fee. And used no chemicals.

Art historians don't just debate modern cleaning methods, they also try to get inside the minds of the masters. One of the most vexing questions about Michelangelo, arguably the best-known sculptor of the Renaissance, is this: Why did he leave so much of his work unfinished? Some of his statues, such as the four *Captives* that line the approach to *David*, were likely meant to remain unfinished because they appear to be struggling to free themselves from the marble blocks.

But other unfinished work cannot be so easily explained. Almost three-quarters of Michelangelo's statues have visible drill holes, chisel marks, and entire sections that are not fully formed. The question has plagued scholars because there isn't an agreed-upon explanation for such unfinished work known as *non finito*, when all that was required in some cases was a few minutes polishing with pumice, water, and straw. The very name of one of his works in the Bargello, *David/Apollo*, indicates no one knows who Michelangelo meant this to be. Is the figure another version of David holding a sling over his shoulder or is this is the Greek god Apollo reaching for an arrow in his quiver?

Michelangelo may have offered a hint about what he was up to on his *Pietà* in St. Peter's in Rome. Once the statue was on view, Michelangelo stood unobtrusively among the pilgrims to hear their comments. In the days before tour guides and descriptive labels, he was chagrined to learn that no one knew whose creation this was so Michelangelo decided he'd better sign the statue. He chiseled on the ribbon that ran across Mary's breast these words in Latin: *Michelangelo Bonarotus Floren. Faciebat.* (Michelangelo Buonarroti of Florence made this.) What's interesting was the tense he used for the verb. He did not use the past tense, *facit*, he used the imperfect, *faciebat*, to indicate that even though he thought the statue was beautiful, the work was not finished. He could make it better any time he wanted, he just did not choose to do so.

The concept of *faciebat* has its own artistic history, a fact that Michelangelo likely knew. Apelles, the court painter for Alexander the Great, signed all his works using that word as an indication that he wasn't done, he had simply decided to stop. Other Renaissance artists followed suit. Titian signed all four hundred of his paintings using the same word. A similar way of thinking was expressed by French poet Paul Valéry when he said, "A poem is never finished, only abandoned."

But the *Pietà* is the only piece that Michelangelo ever signed. If he had that ancient tradition in mind, why did he not use the same resonant word elsewhere? According to some accounts, *Brutus*, the only bust Michelangelo ever made, is unfinished because he was summoned by the pope to carry out an important commission. Yet the parts of Brutus that are unfinished, the hair and the ears, could never have been completed because Michelangelo didn't leave enough marble.

To understand how this might happen, imagine you're lying in a bath. Someone pulls the plug and your naked body slowly appears as the water drains away. First to show might be a raised knee, or a pair of breasts in the case of a woman, then a hand, and so on. That's how Michelangelo chiseled and hammered his way to the finished product, working from front to back in order to create a three-dimensional shape from the original block of marble. How likely is it that the master got to the back of Brutus's head and realized to his horror that he'd forgotten about the ears on the way by?

As Michelangelo grew older and more celebrated, his ego got oversized. He claimed he'd never learned anything in the workshops of others; he'd had no mentors, no teachers. He claimed that his talent was a gift from God and he was a divine being, that's why he was so good. In the last days before his death, Michelangelo destroyed hundreds of his preliminary drawings because he did not want the world to know the effort that went into each statue. We were supposed to believe that the final vision sprang full-blown from his brow rather than after dozens of sketches showing different possible body positions.

Various explanations have been offered for what art historian Frederick Hartt called Michelangelo's "strange artistic paralysis." Some claim he simply was too busy to worry about finishing since he wanted to go on to the next work and was able to create a buzz by being in such demand. Perhaps he wanted the viewer to see the hand of the artist, to appreciate that he had started with nothing, and created something out of that nothing. Or maybe this was all about human frailty and the fear of dying. If there still was work to do then he could have an eternal life right here on earth.

I'm not sure I can come up with a new explanation for the long-standing question about "unfinished." But this much I do know. The reason this topic is fascinating is because his *non finito* work is the very root of modern art. Michelangelo was not necessarily the best sculptor of his time. I agree with artist Robert Morris, who has said, "For me Renaissance sculpture stops with Donatello." But Michelangelo is better known and more honored than all the rest because his work still has relevance.

Modern art requires some viewer participation. We don't need to be told the whole story; we like to fill in the blanks. Michelangelo's unfinished sculpture allows that sort of viewer involvement. His *Pitti Tondo* is all about the Christ child's joy and the Madonna's melancholy look, as if she knows this moment will not last. Michelangelo communicates their emotion without any need to finish her right hand that cuddles the baby, the facial features of St. John, or anything in the background.

The reason for *non finito* isn't as important as the result. Michelangelo was not just a sculptor of the Renaissance, but a creative force with eternal appeal. What more could an artist want? What more could we hope to experience? We look and we not only see, but we also feel and we know. Across the ages, that's more than enough.

❖

The sun is up as we leave the apartment at 6:30 a.m., a welcome change from a few weeks back when it was pitch black at this hour. Pink clouds hang in the sky, lit by the rising sun; an overnight rain has infused the air with the unmistakable scent of spring. Yesterday at San Miniato al Monte, high above Florence, we saw the first sure signs of the new season – apple trees afroth with delicate white blossoms, a touch of yellow at the throat.

Today's destinations are Parma and Mantova, two cities in Lombardy, each of them home to powerful women during the Renaissance. While each woman was very different from the other, both were extraordinary in an era of male dominance. Parma, famous for its ham and parmesan cheese, was the early sixteenth-century site of the Benedictine convent of San Paolo. Giovanna da Piacenza, abbess of the nunnery and a close friend of Pope Leo X, was granted an exemption by him to turn her cloistered life into a literary salon where she invited the intelligentsia to conduct lively debate and artistic pursuits.

To this yeasty place in 1519 came Antonio Allegri, the painter later known as Correggio, named after his nearby hometown. Then thirty years old, he may have traveled to Rome to see the works of Raphael and Michelangelo, or he may have been self-taught, no one knows for sure. What is certain is that under the patronage of Giovanna da Piacenza he painted in a soft, sweet, and original baroque style that was one hundred years ahead of its time.

Correggio created a gazebo in Giovanna's bedroom, *Camera di San Paolo*, by painting the thin ribs of the domed ceiling to look like bamboo surrounded by fruit, playful putti, and allegorical panels. One goddess depicted is Io, the wife of Jupiter. He fooled around, she did not, but he punished her anyway so she is shown hanging with golden anvils tied to her feet. Giovanna herself is represented as Diana, goddess of the hunt. Carved above the fireplace is her Latin motto, which translates as "Don't poke the fire with a sword." In other words, yes, there is freedom to say whatever you want in this room, but don't push me too far, I'm still the boss.

Born of a noble family, Giovanna's rebellious court's time in the bright sunshine of intellectual stimulation was relatively short, about a dozen years. When Leo X died he was replaced in 1522 by the only Dutch-born pope, Adrian VI, who shut down the convent, much to the satisfaction of others in the Church who had been complaining about her unusual lifestyle.

By then Correggio had won other commissions in Parma, including the *Vision of St. John the Evangelist* in the dome of San Giovanni Evangelista as well as what became regarded as his finest work, the *Assumption of the Virgin*, painted in the dome of the cathedral of Parma. To portray the frescoed figures using foreshortening, which was required for viewing from below, he suspended small sculptures on wire, made sketches, and then transferred his drawings to the vault. No bodily position is repeated among the tumultuous panorama of more than 350 sensuous figures.

As Correggio's fame spread, his work attracted other great artists. Among the pilgrims was Titian who stared in silence for a long time at Correggio's *Assumption*. Finally a member of his entourage screwed up enough courage to ask the maestro for his thoughts. "Get a big saw and cut that dome away. Then turn it upside down, fill it with gold, and it will not be enough," said

Titian. Without Giovanna da Piacenza's unlikely convent launch pad, Correggio might never have been discovered. He died at forty-four, walking to his hometown on a hot summer's day.

In nearby Mantova lived another woman of substance who had an even greater impact on today's art world. Isabella d'Este, wife of Francesco Gonzaga, Marquis of Mantova, was born in 1475. Intelligent and beautiful, she had blond hair and blue eyes, studied Greek and Latin, played the lute, and composed sonnets. But Isabella's most notable talent was her eye for art and artists. Among those who visited her at the five-hundred-room Palazzo Ducale was Leonardo da Vinci, who painted her portrait and advised on some vases she'd acquired. With the help of her refined taste and knowledgeable eye, the Gonzaga family built the world's largest art museum consisting of two thousand paintings – including thirty-six Titians – as well as twenty thousand sculptures and other items.

Unlike other collectors of the time, such as the Medicis who for the most part promoted local artists, her vision was more extensive: Peter Paul Rubens, Andrea Mantegna, Giulio Romano, and Tintoretto. Female artists also held pride of place and did work that was avant-garde. For example, Lavinia Fontana painted a woman wearing a court dress but with a face covered in fur. Isabella had a special room, known as a *studiolo*, with a writing desk where she would receive artists and view objects from her own collection.

Isabella became known as *la prima donna del mondo*, the first woman of the world, but her renown went beyond the cultural. At one point, after her husband was captured, she took command of his troops and ordered them to defend the city against the enemy rather than surrender. The strength of her example and her steadfast strategy succeeded.

There was also a bizarre side to the family: the Gonzaga line loved midgets. A midget appears in a fresco by Andrea Mantegna, done for what became the *Camera degli Sposi* (Wedding Chamber) of Isabella and Francesco. What started out as a few pet midgets at court grew to such a number that an apartment, appropriate to their diminutive size, was built for them in the palace. Today, their lodgings are not open to tourists, but you can peer through a doorway covered by an iron gate to get an idea of the lavish life led by the little people and the honor in which they were held.

Isabella outlived her husband and ruled until 1539 when she died in her mid-sixties. Almost a century later, the dynasty went bankrupt. All the art except the frescoes, which could not be moved, was sold to Charles I of England. After Charles was hanged, Oliver Cromwell put everything up for auction. So great was the number and quality of the Gonzaga collection that it formed the basis for three of the most famous museums in the world: the Louvre in Paris, the Prado in Madrid, and the Kunsthistorisches in Vienna.

As we leave Mantova in the early evening, the sliver of a crescent moon hangs on its back in the sky above the windows of Isabella's bedroom and *studiolo* as it did in her day. Just as great artists can achieve immortality through their work, so, too, can patrons like Isabelle d'Este and Giovanna da Piacenza gain renown and remain celebrated long after their time on this earth has come and gone.

Paolo Penco is a meticulous man who sports a goatee and wears a dress shirt and tie while working at his jeweler's bench around the corner from the Duomo. His design ideas not only flow directly from the Renaissance, but he has also resurrected methods from those times that had previously fallen from favor or been abandoned. At fifteen, after Paolo finished middle school, he took a five-year program at the Art Institute of Porta Romana and received his Diploma of Master of Art. The first three years were general study and during the final two he specialized in goldsmithing.

Paolo read about the Renaissance, visited museums to view the art, and studied the skills of artisans. "There were some goldsmiths in Florence but most of the techniques had been lost. I wanted to bring back those practices where the finished product is a bearer of culture." Paolo is a descendent of a noble Hungarian family that moved to Florence in the eighteenth century following in the footsteps of the new sovereigns of the Grand Duchy of Tuscany: Francis II of Lorena and his wife Mary Theresa of Austria. Paolo's father and grandfather sold coins, stamps, and jewelry, none of which was handmade. Because there was no teacher with whom to study, no workshop where he could sign on as an apprentice, Paolo turned to the writings of Benvenuto Cellini, the sixteenth-century sculptor and goldsmith. In 1554 Cellini wrote *Opere* (Works) a book of almost 1,100 pages that describes his flamboyant life and includes some of his poetry as well as his secret methods.

After Paolo opened his goldsmith's workshop in 1985, when he was twenty years old, he experimented with Cellini's explanations, particularly one called *niello*, a way of decorating engraved metal using an alloy. To create the alloy Paolo melts silver, copper, and lead in a crucible and then pours the liquid into a terra cotta urn containing powdered sulfur. Even the urn's dimensions follow Cellini's description – "the size of the man's hand." The sulfur quickly burns off, revealing the black alloy, which is then formed into sticks that can be re-melted as required.

To create a finished piece, Paolo heats a stick and pours the liquid alloy into cold water where it becomes granules the same size as grains of rice – again following Cellini's description. The surface of the object, such as a locket, is engraved by hand using a sharp, pointed tool called a *bulino*. The granules are ground with a mortar and pestle and then reheated to create a paste for application onto an etched and polished surface. Time taken on an individual piece can be anywhere from one to three days but even then, if he is not satisfied with the result, Paolo will start again. "Five hundred years of inspiration," he says with a laugh, "it's simple."

Paolo Penco's shop on Via Ferdinand Zannetti is called Penko, using the original spelling of the family name before it was Italianized after unification in 1870. In addition to his work in *niello*, Paolo also designs and makes ornate gold and silver jewelry. Typical is a long necklace in yellow 18K gold with two large Australian pearls and nine carats of sapphires that's a copy of the necklace worn by the woman in Pontormo's painting *Lady with a Dog* and costs 12,653 euros, or about C$20,000.

Paolo has fifteen employees, but he does 60 per cent of the work on each piece himself. Employees build the basic structure, piercing the metal to create designs or the settings for stones, but he selects the gems and does all of the finishing work. He is selective about custom orders. "If a customer asks me to make something I don't like, I don't make it." Barneys in New York carries some of his pieces, such as a dragonfly brooch that sells for US$6,125, three times what Paolo charges the upscale retailer.

Working with the *niello* technique is the most time-consuming of Paolo's creations and is therefore the most expensive. The highest-priced *niello* piece Paolo has ever made, a pocket watch, took three months of labor over a two-year period. He charged his Japanese client 50 million lire, or about 26,000 euros. "I am the only one who does this work today because it takes so long. If you consider the time the object takes, you have to do it to maintain the old tradition and for the love of the work. I am an artisan with passion."

Despite Cellini's lengthy specifics, some of the master's descriptions are discreetly incomplete. "It's a difficult process and there are a lot of secrets. I can see what's needed because of experience," says Paolo. One of the more enigmatic sentences in

Cellini's book reads, *Io non ho detto alla metà di quel che importa a quest'arte, che veramenta la vuole tutto un uomo* which translates as "I have told only half of what is important to learn this trade, that truly wants all of a man." In other words, Cellini can take even the most willing student only so far, the rest must be discovered through aptitude and experiment, patience and practice.

❖

There is no plaque, but Wolfgang Amadeus Mozart lived a few doors away from Paolo Penco's shop on the two occasions when the young prodigy visited Florence with his father, Leopold. The historic marker that does hang on the façade celebrates a poetess instead, Maria Maddelena Morelli, known as Corilla. The carved tablet on the house where Michelangelo grew up on Via dei Bentaccordia, near Santa Croce, does not mention that his father beat him daily when he was a boy. The artist Raphael lived from 1504 to 1508 at 15 Via Giorni, but the historic plaque is elsewhere. A recent owner of the palazzo decided he did not want gawkers and was able to obtain the necessary permission to have the tablet, as well as a tabernacle he did not like, moved to nearby Via Taddea. Donatello once lived where Via Roma is today, but the street had another name that disappeared as part of a massive urban renewal project that began when Italy was being unified in 1865 and Florence was designated to be the capital.

For a time under the Medicis, Jews were prized and could live wherever they wanted, although most chose to live near the synagogue south of the Arno. They were moneylenders and doctors, and they participated in cloth production and trade. In 1570, their freedom ended when Cosimo I ordered Jews to live in a ghetto near the Mercato Vecchio (Old Market) behind iron gates that were locked at night. Civic leaders decided to level the slums in preparation for the arrival of government officials and a surge in population. About twenty-five thousand civil servants did come to Florence and then decamped just as quickly for Rome when that city was named as the capital in 1870.

Florence decided to push ahead with the massive downtown renewal plan anyway. Nothing of historic value, from sixteenth-century buildings to the foundations of the old Roman city, was saved. The only protests came from foreigners. An article in the *New York Times* resulted in thousands of signatures collected in the United States, France, Germany, and England. The locals did not listen. The Old Market was replaced by Piazza della Repubblica; the Jews moved east and built a fine new synagogue of Moorish design. The Holy Ark still bears the bayonet marks made by the Fascists in the 1930s. The Nazis used the synagogue as a garage and put to death 248 Florentine Jews whose names are listed on a wall outside the synagogue.

On the west side of Repubblica stands an enormous triumphal arch, erected in 1895, with the carved words *L'antico centro della città de secolare squallore a vita nuova restituto* (The ancient centre of the city, squalid for centuries, restored to a new life). The project remained controversial as late as 1970 when Edoardo Detti published a book called *Florence That Was*. "Until the mid-nineteenth century Florence was essentially a medieval city," he wrote. "The destruction of the old centre has been unanimously and persistently called the greatest crime of the last century." New streets were built and old ones straightened to create a grid pattern that gave no thought to any "artful visual perspective."

The former Via dell'Arcivescovado was renamed Via Roma. Our apartment, erected in 1929, was one of the last of the new structures in the redeveloped area. Some buildings in the vicinity were done in the flamboyant Liberty style of architecture, Italy's version of Art Nouveau. While Via Roma 3 enjoys few of those exterior elements – fanciful animals, female faces, and elaborate wrought iron – we do have ceramic floor tiles that reflect the Liberty floral motifs.

The next architectural phase in Florence was far more brutal than the renewal project. The Santa Maria Novella train station, built in the 1930s by Mussolini's Fascists, was among the first structures in what became known as the National style. The flat-roofed, three-storey, yellow-brick building is stark and relentless, with no redeeming features. Obviously, I never saw the destroyed buildings, except in old photographs. To my mind, little was lost. The current streetscape, although not medieval, is elegant and the piazzas are lively places.

On March 10, three months to the day since we last sat outside at Gilli, it is warm enough to do so again. That day in December it was 20°C; today it is only 13°C, but against the wall in the mid-afternoon sun it is warm enough to have a drink and watch the world go by in Piazza della Repubblica. A young couple who look like newlyweds finish their drink and climb into an open carriage for the horse-drawn tour. She looks so happy; he appears so proud. They are accompanied by their dog, a golden Labrador. If a dog can smile, he is doing so, and looks delighted to be along. Some things have not changed since December. A man I call Lothario still trolls the piazza searching for discarded women of a certain age. He is maybe fifty-five, with dyed black hair, and wears his cashmere topcoat unbuttoned to reveal his pulsing manhood trapped in tight-fitting jeans. He saunters with hands clasped behind his back, shoulders swinging this way and that, as he smiles and scans the faces. He picks out a pair of well-heeled ladies seated outside at Gilli, one in a green silk jacket and the other wearing a smart black hat. He stops to make conversation over the low hedge that separates the café tables from the street.

At first, they seem pleased to have been selected; they draw back their shoulders to show themselves off to best advantage. He rocks on his feet, gesticulating with one hand, giving his best bravura performance. After two or three minutes, their shoulders sag just a little, they stop making an effort to look fetching, and they return to sipping their colored drinks through tiny straws. He carries on for another minute in a last-gasp effort to recapture their attention, and then nods politely and slithers away, looking for fresh faces. The ladies may not have liked him very much but back home they will tell their bridge club friends about this flirtatious Florentine encounter. He *was sooo cute*, they will say, roll their eyes, toss back their heads, and give a throaty laugh.

Lothario is replaced by a gypsy wearing a headscarf who

rattles her paltry few coins in a proffered paper cup. Men on the make might be allowed, but Gilli is off limits to beggars. A white-jacketed waiter scurries over, clapping his hands as if she were a pigeon to be shooed away. A man in a short-sleeved shirt who may be in the wrong city reads a guidebook about Venice. An American couple meets up with friends at a nearby table. "I bought a leather coat at the market. It's the last thing I wanted," announces the man who has just arrived. "It cost one hundred and eighty euros but I got it for ninety." No praise flows from his friends so I sneak a peek at his purchase. The coat is moss green with bilious yellow undertones. Good leather should be supple, but this looks stiff, like armor. Across the back, excess material forms a large bubble like a turtle's shell. You just know when he gets home the coat will hang at the back of the closet, unworn, and he will wonder why he bothered.

A tour group straggles by, their guide speaking softly into a headset, the visitors listening to her patter on individual earphones. Tourism has gone high-tech wireless. Fewer bullhorn explanations mean we can more easily hear Piotr Tomaszewski, the Polish classical guitarist who strums in the piazza daily. He must be nearing the end of his set. He is playing one of his usual closing numbers, Eric Clapton's "Tears in Heaven," the one with the words, "Would you know my name if I saw you in Heaven." But aren't we already there?

Holy Week, the seven days before Easter, begins on Palm Sunday with leafy olive branches presented to passersby outside the Duomo. Just before the 11 a.m. service a gowned ecclesiastical parade carries tall palm fronds through the front doors into the church. The city's gardens are coming alive with bloom: hyacinth, daffodils, magnolia, flowering almond, and mimosa. The sidewalks of Via Roma are ablaze with pink azaleas in large terra cotta tubs.

The tourists have returned; throngs again fill Piazza del Duomo. Since November, any time I looked, there would be only one tour group hearing a guide's spiel below our window. This week there are four to six such clusters at any given moment. After living here for more than six months I can understand something of how the Florentines must feel about the annual invasion of fair-weather visitors. Just who *are* these interlopers who clog intersections trying to decipher maps or block sidewalks as they walk slowly in open-mouthed amazement? Well, in the words of the *memento mori*, the skeleton lying at the base of Masaccio's *Trinity* in Santa Maria Novella, "You are what I was and I am what you will become."

On Monday, in that same church, we attend a presentation of Requiem KV 626, the musical score Mozart was writing in 1791 when he died. The requiem, commissioned by an anonymous patron and well known because of the film *Amadeus*, has become one of the most-performed pieces of religious music and is particularly popular at this time of year. Many local churches present versions of this mass, but we picked this 9 p.m. concert not only because the interior of the church is beautiful, but also because the poster promised that the event was *ingresso libero*, free.

Many others have been drawn by the same allure. Seating for five hundred is quickly filled; another five hundred sit on the floor in the center aisle or stand at the sides of the church throughout the ninety-minute performance. Two magnificent crucifixes serve as reminders why we are here in these four-teenth-century surroundings: one carved by Brunelleschi hangs to the left of the altar, the other, painted by Giotto, is suspended over our heads. The concert is magnificent, the four soloists mighty.

Beside us are the proud parents of twenty-year-old Gaia Gioli who has been playing the viola since she was seven. She attends the Music School of Fiesole and is part of the forty-member orchestra that's accompanied by a sixty-voice choir. We learn that ever since music programs were eliminated from public schools, interested students must attend private schools, an expensive undertaking. Her university education will also be costly. In Italy, tuition fees are geared to family income, but that means declared income, so a plumber who receives cash for his work will not pay as much for his child's tuition as someone on salary who cannot hide income. Even doctors have opportunities to earn cash, telling patients that if they need an invoice for an office visit, the fee will be one hundred euros, but if they pay cash, the charge is only fifty euros.

Beyond the unfairness of such a system, the Giolis say that only because they live in a city the size of Florence where there is a local university, can their daughter and son continue their education by living at home. Going away to school would mean having to take an apartment, an impossible expense. Like par-

ents everywhere, they worry about prospects for their offspring. Too few jobs are available for graduates. The Middle
Ages remain visible in Florence, but is the modern era viable?
"We have worked hard," says Gaia's mother, "but the world
our parents gave us was better than the world we are giving to
our children."

Easter celebrations reach a crescendo on Sunday at the Duomo.
Beginning at 10 a.m. there is a procession along Via Roma of the
now familiar medieval costumes, drummers, trumpeters, and
flag-tossers as well as official representatives from the police,
church, and city. What makes this parade different from all the
others is the *carro*, a huge wooden cart that's about ten meters
high and looks oriental in design. The cart, which is loaded
with fireworks, was pulled in the past by two white oxen but
the beasts have become mostly symbolic. All the hard work to
position the cart strategically between the Baptistery and the
Duomo has been done by a farm tractor.

With so many members of the media on hand, the mayor
takes the opportunity to hold an impromptu news conference.
Local elections are less than ten days away; every bit of expo-
sure helps. As we watch proceedings from our rooftop terrace
high above the crush of the crowd, we drink glasses of bellini
and listen to the bells of Giotto's Campanile. According to
legend, this ceremony of the exploding cart celebrates the
exploits of Pazzino de' Pazzi, an eleventh-century Florentine
warrior from the First Crusade. As the first man to climb the

walls of Jericho he was awarded two pieces of stone from the Holy Sepulcher, the shards of which are still used to start a fire that is carried through the streets to light the fireworks. If all goes well, everyone will enjoy good luck and good crops this year.

At precisely 11 a.m., accompanied by more pealing of bells, inside the church the archbishop lights a dove-shaped rocket, the *colombina*, which is sent flying on a wire out through the church door where it ignites the fireworks on the cart, then immediately turns around and scoots back inside. For the next ten minutes, roman candles, katy wheels, various rockets and screamers bang and howl in red, green, yellow, and blue, soaring as high as the top of the church façade while shimmering silver confetti falls above the heads of the delighted crowd. Small boys wonder why church isn't like this every week as the good luck flows all around.

APRIL

AS WE RETURN FROM DINNER on Saturday, April 2, we stop to watch a mime charm an audience of three hundred on the street. We've seen him before, but the routine is always worth watching. The man, dressed like Charlie Chaplin, picks three people from the crowd, usually a ten-year-old boy, a twenty-something woman, and a fifty-ish man. Using only body language and a police whistle, he directs them to do silly things like look through their legs, play-act different roles, and generally make fools of themselves to much merriment among the gathering. Suddenly, church bells begin to toll. Never before have we heard bells at 10 p.m. but we know exactly what the somber sound means. *Il Papa è morto*. The pope is dead. A week ago John Paul II did not participate in Easter Sunday services for the first time in his twenty-six years as the bishop of Rome. Since then the litany of his internal problems has grown longer; all day he has been slipping in and out of consciousness.

Two blocks away a crowd gathers on the steps of the

Duomo. Some stand with heads bowed, others lift their faces toward Heaven. For the most part, everyone is silent, lost in thought about the man, his death, and his life. Few words are exchanged but the one phrase that keeps being repeated is *santo subito*, immediate sainthood, their hope for his speedy beatification.

Newscasts confirm what the streets already knew: his Holiness, the first non-Italian pope in 450 years, died at 9:37 p.m. He was eighty-four. As we watch the live television coverage of the hushed crowd in St. Peter's Square, we feel strangely connected to the saddened masses. We had stood in St. Peter's less than two months ago and looked up at the same three windows of the pope's rooms in the Vatican, the focus of so much sorrowful attention this night. The Sistine Chapel that we visited will be the scene later this month of the conclave when cardinals gather from more than fifty countries to select one from among their number who next will wear the shoes of the fisherman.

Maybe it's because we have been living in Italy, where 85 per cent of the population is Catholic, but the pope's death takes on more significance for us than it otherwise might. Since February when he was hospitalized we have been watching his slow deterioration, as he became, in the words of a Vatican spokesman, "a soul pulling a body." The Church may not have the same strong hold on its flock of 1.1 billion followers as it once did but this pope was special. He was the first pope to visit a synagogue and a mosque. He decried apartheid, helped topple Communism, and opposed the war in Iraq. In a world with too few values, he was a moral leader. He visited 129 countries, spreading the gospel, particularly among the young.

A little more than two weeks later, I'm writing at my desk when I realize that the bells of Giotto's Campanile have been ringing for a minute or so. In itself, that's not an unusual event; they always peal at 5:30 p.m. but isn't it a little later? I check the time in the upper right-hand corner of my laptop screen: 6:12 p.m. There can only be one meaning to this joyous sound: *Habemus Papam*, "We have a pope." I turn on the TV and watch the smoke billowing from the chimney of the Sistine Chapel. The smoke had begun about 6 p.m. but there was confusion for a while. Was it white? Was it black? Was it gray? When the bells of St. Peter's began ringing at 6:04 p.m., the world could be certain that the 115 cardinals had, in the second day of their conclave, chosen a new pope. The bells outside our window joined the celebration maybe six minutes later, marking the second time this month that the tolling of bells has delivered the news, an unusual means of communication in this electronic age. German-born Joseph Cardinal Ratzinger, now Benedict XVI, is quickly given an Italian nickname – Papa Ratzi.

On the night of John Paul II's demise we have some special visitors who are particular reminders to us that life goes on, family life in particular. Our son Mark, his wife Andrea, and our five-month-old granddaughter Molly arrived thirty-six hours earlier from Toronto. The idea had come up only a week before, proof that frequent-flyer points do sometimes work. I held Molly for the first time during my book tour shortly after she was born last October; Sandy and I spent time with her at

Christmas when we were home; and we were looking forward to seeing her in May, so this surprise trip is a bonus. Molly is all things bright and beautiful. Passersby in Florence break into smiles when they see her, women cross the street to stop us, admire her at close range, touch her outstretched hand, and whisper *bellissima*.

We take them to Santa Maria Novella and Santissima Annunziata as well as some favorite museums, Museo dell'Opera and the Bargello, where Sandy gives a reprise of her talk last month to fellow students about Michelangelo. Molly and I go for a ride on the carrousel in Repubblica and I sneak her a taste of gelato when Mommy's not looking. Molly licks her lips and her eyes grow round – *panna con amerano* is a favorite flavor of mine, too.

At dinner on that Saturday night of the pope's death, Leo, the third generation of his family to run Ristorante Leo near the church of Santa Croce, fusses over Molly. Mark and Andrea ate here on their honeymoon in 2001 and now are back with their baby. Leo cradles Molly in his arms and carries her to the kitchen to show her a photo of Joya, his daughter of eight months, his first girl after five sons with three wives. The chef visits our table twice to boast about his eight-month-old daughter who weighs ten kilos, two kilos more than Joya. "How much does Molly weigh? Does she have any teeth yet?" Food, family, and friends – the three ingredients that make life in this country so unique – offer contentment and continuity despite a pope's passing.

❖

On the crest of a hill on the southern edge of Florence sits a fourteenth-century monastery that was occupied by the Carthusian monks until 1955. A twenty-minute ride on city bus 37 and a ten-minute amble takes you up to the Certosa del Galluzzo (Charterhouse) and another world. The eighteen members of this radical order lived as hermits, their lives devoted to prayer and meditation. Don't, however, imagine them kneeling in dark, tiny, and windowless cells. Think instead of a row of elegant townhouses, each with a living room, bedroom, study area, and large L-shaped walled garden into which their neighbor monks could not look. Lay brothers left food daily in wall boxes with interior access, the original meals on wheels. French architect Le Corbusier visited several times to study the architectural design of the monastery with its three cloistered gardens and grand views of the Tuscan countryside.

Such was the solitude of their lives that the monks talked with each other just twice a week for an hour each time. Once was at the shared Sunday meal, the other was in the *parlatorio*, a narrow hallway with a long bench on both walls. Days could pass before a death was discovered and only then after someone had peered through a peephole into the bedroom, since entry to the living quarters was not permitted even under the most suspicious of circumstances. A waiting list to join the order meant that no suite of rooms remained empty for long.

It was here in 1522 that the artist Pontormo fled to escape the plague that was sweeping Florence. The pestilence would arrive every few years without warning, spread by black rats.

The first symptom for victims was the swelling of the lymph nodes in the thighs or armpits. The lumps, filled with pus, were called buboes, thus the name bubonic plague. Treatment ranged from potions and bloodletting to prayers and penitence, but nothing worked. Death usually came within a week, sooner if the disease reached the lungs. Sputum and coughing guaranteed the spread of the airborne germs until the plague mercifully waned just as mysteriously as it had arrived.

The Doge of Venice, who believed that the disease was spread by travelers from the Orient, ordered new arrivals to be isolated for the same period of time as Christ spent in the wilderness – forty days, *quaranta giorni* – thus the origin of the word *quarantine*. A sanctuary such as a monastery, where there was limited contact with the outside world, offered the best chance of avoiding the death sentence that regularly came to millions across Europe. As thanks and payment for the two years he stayed with the Carthusians, Pontormo painted five frescoes showing scenes in the life of Christ from the moment before his betrayal by Judas in the Garden of Gethsemane to the deposition from the cross. Pontormo's style was unique: elongated bodies, small heads, and vibrant colors in pinks, greens, and purples.

The Certosa has been occupied since 1958 by the Cistercians who charge one euro per person for a guided tour of the premises and sell their high-octane liqueurs in a shop. Every visitor probably poses the same question: Could I live here? At first it seems like an appealing existence, peaceful and problem-free, with nothing to do but pray, read, ponder life, and tend a few tomatoes. But for how long? A one-week holiday, a two-week retreat, twenty-eight days to quit drinking? And then what? A lifetime of silent contemplation might be a tad too long.

Most monks of the Middle Ages who lived in similar surroundings were anonymous souls who left no mark. That's not the case for St. Francis of Assisi, patron saint of Italy. Two days after our visit to Certosa di Firenze, we go on the trail of the world's most famous friar. Our first stop in Assisi, 150 kilometers south of Florence in Umbria, is Santa Maria degli Angeli, the basilica built in the seventeenth century where St. Francis died. Before we're even inside, we're swept up in the combination of religious reverence and crass commercialism that surrounds St. Francis today. After an earthquake in 1997 devastated the region, the golden statue of the Madonna of the Angels was taken down from the top of the church for repairs. One night, a local man noticed that the shadow cast by the statue on the church wall looked exactly like St. Francis in his hooded robes. He took a photo and ever since members of the family have been selling prints of the minor miracle at 1.50 euro each.

Born in 1181 into the family of a prosperous merchant, Francesco Bernadone had olive skin, dark hair, dark eyes, and called himself the "black chicken." He designed his own clothes and was a playboy whose money paid for so many parties that his friends dubbed him "King of Feasts." One day when he was in San Damiano, then a small, abandoned church in the woods, he heard the voice of God saying, "Go, rebuild my church, which is falling into ruin."

Did He mean the spiritual or the physical, the chapel or the entire church hierarchy? At first, St. Francis, twenty-six, took the words literally and repaired the chapel, and then he started his own religious order followed by two more in Assisi where the religious community remains sizable. Nowhere in Italy, not even in Rome, are there so many priests and nuns in the streets wearing robes and rope sashes with the three knots representing poverty, chastity, and obedience.

The business of St. Francis has become a thriving industry. Three million visitors annually come to Assisi to worship and see the saint's garment and sandals. At his tomb, we saw a friar respectfully replacing six partially consumed candles with new ones; he handed the still smoking stubs to pilgrims who solemnly accepted the surprise souvenir.

Next stop is back north towards Florence then up a switch-back road to La Verna at the top of a mountain, thirteen hundred meters above sea level, where in 1224 St. Francis came to pray and fast in the hopes of having a mystical experience. On the fortieth day of his deprivation St. Francis had a vision of the crucified Christ. When he awoke, he had received the five wounds of the cross, one in each hand and each foot as if from the nails, one in his side from the soldier's lance.

The condition is called stigmata, and St. Francis was not particularly pleased to have been so honored. From a practical standpoint, the wounds were painful; he needed special shoes with holes in the soles so he could walk. He wore gloves to hide the wounds and told his disciples to keep the stigmata secret. Only after he died two years later, when his body was washed in preparation for burial, did others learn what happened. News of the stigmata spread quickly and gave him special status; he was made a saint within two years, a speed record that still stands.

In the modern era, hundreds of individuals claim to have received similar wounds. The Catholic Church refuses to become involved in deciding who is telling the truth and who is a fraud seeking publicity. Medical proof is required to show that the wounds do not heal and do not become infected, two essential criteria. In the twentieth century there were 137 documented cases of stigmata. Of those, 88 – almost two-thirds – were women, including 36 from religious orders. Italy had the most with 51, France was next with 23, and there were 5 in Canada.

The best-known was Padre Pio, who received the five visible wounds in 1918 as a young Capuchin priest in San Giovanni Rotondo, Italy. Until his death in 1968, the wounds were open and would regularly ooze blood with a perfumed fragrance. Over the years, thousands of people came to hear him say mass, receive confession, or touch his mittened hands in the hopes he could heal their ailments. The Church, fearing a personality cult, for a time limited Padre Pio's public duties.

The Church was equally worried about St. Francis. After his death officials altered events of his life so the outspoken rebel was rendered meek and mild. For example, after a visit to Rome when St. Francis was shocked by the luxurious lifestyle of the pope and his cardinals, he called for avenging birds to attack them. The Church rewrote the story, turning the birds into sparrows feeding at his feet, and so was born the modern-day image. Today, two white doves roost in a hallway at Santa Maria degli Angeli as symbols of that affinity with animals. La Verna, the site of a Franciscan monastery, is more restrained and less commercial than Assisi. The views from the precipice are spectacular, the warblers sing in the woods, and a plaque marks the spot where St. Francis received the stigmata. For six euros the friars serve travelers a hearty evening meal of spaghetti with ragu sauce and some red wine.

The entryway to the cave where St. Francis slept almost eight hundred years ago is so narrow that passage is restricted to one person at a time. During his visit, David Pellettier, the winter term's coordinator of OCAD's Florence program, noticed that drips of water on the rock wall had formed a dark and life-sized likeness of St. Francis with his hands raised in prayer. After he told me, we went back together later so he could show me the image. I made a quick sketch in my notebook but we took no photo, we have no image for sale. Better to let the priest remain a source of inspiration than be the basis for profit.

✻

Stefano Bemer's hands are flattened, palms down, floating barely above the piece of tanned hide that's spread on his workroom table as if he is a healer seeking someone's aura. As a maker of men's custom shoes Stefano is deciding precisely where he will cut this piece of leather to create the uppers. The specific areas he selects must not only look attractive as individual shoes but also be perfect together as a matched pair.

He particularly likes this fissured piece of hide because it comes from the neck of a cow. "There is more movement in this area of the animal than elsewhere so there are creases and folds that make for interesting patterns," he says, his body swaying in sync with his hands, until he stops at an area that to my untrained eye looks no different from any other. "Here, here is where I will cut."

A walk around Stefano's workshop is like a tour of the globe, with its stacks of hides from the best tanneries: Tannerie d'Annonay in Annonay, France; Charles F. Stead in Leeds, England; and Horween Leather in Chicago, which specializes in cordovan that takes six months to cure. He also shows me a dozen types of exotic skins: sharkskin from Mexico and the China Sea; kudu, hippo, crocodile, ostrich, and elephant from Africa; yellow frog from Australia; stomachs from who knows where; and a vintage sealskin that's sixteen years old.

You want older? He has Russian reindeer hide recovered in 1973 from the *Catherina von Flensburg*, a Danish vessel that sank off the coast of Plymouth, England, in 1786. The hide has been re-tanned using eighteenth-century methods and comes complete with a certificate of authenticity. Skins he uses from animals such as elephant, crocodile, and hippo are subject to an international agreement, the Convention on International Trade in Endangered Species, so that the wearer can be assured that the animal died of natural causes and was not killed for the skin

or the tusks or the sport. "The research of materials is my obses-
sion. When you get the quality, the price is not important," he
says.

Stefano, forty, is almost elfin in size, has tousled brown hair,
a full beard, and a cheery disposition on a boyish face. Even
when he is standing, he appears to be slightly hunched, as if
he's just risen from his cobbler's bench and would rather be
back at work. At nineteen, after completing school and compul-
sory military service, he was living with his parents in Greve in
Chianti, wondering what to do with his life. A heel on his shoe
needed mending and he discovered that Greve, population six
thousand, had no shoemaker. His best friend had just started
working for a Mr. Minute shoe repair franchise in a nearby
town, so while Stefano got his shoe fixed, he watched his friend
work, and then he bought some of the necessary instruments to
try the trade himself.

Stefano rented space in Greve and held a grand opening
with a special offer to fix one pair of shoes per customer for free.
He was inundated. "I had the workshop but no experience. I
closed the shop for fifteen days and stayed inside to learn how
to repair shoes." He sought out a sympathetic shoemaker in
Florence who showed him the basics and oversaw Stefano's
early work.

After three years, he opened a shop in the San Frediano district of Florence south of the Arno River. He did some simple
repairs for a wealthy client who invited him to dinner and
showed Stefano his closets filled with 120 pairs of made-to-
measure shoes, from John Lobb of London and Gatto in Rome,

all organized by style and color. "It was a fantastic collection, all shining and beautiful. When I saw those I wanted to make beautiful shoes."

To do so, he repaired shoes during the day and then spent three hours every evening with a retired custom shoemaker who was willing to share what he knew. Once Stefano knew how to take proper foot measurements, construct a shoe, and modify the last, he split his time – two days a week making custom shoes and four days on repairs to earn a living. "At first my work wasn't very good so I couldn't charge much. Customers would come with photos of shoes they liked and wanted made. I'd say 'Okay' and we'd select the materials. When the customer left the shop I'd say to myself, 'I'm crazy, I don't know how to make these shoes.' I was embarrassed that I couldn't make them exactly the way they wanted." Today Stefano has a dozen employees, two shops in Florence and one in Tokyo. He has three lines of shoes: in the least expensive line a pair costs 500 euros and uses top-quality leather but involves some machine work and a Goodyear sole; a pair of shoes in his prêt-à-porter line costs 750 to 825 euros; at the top, the first pair of bespoke shoes fetches 1,800 euros and requires forty hours of work spread over three months. Once the last has been made, successive pairs cost 1,550 euros each (about C$2,500). "Thirty pairs of handmade shoes will last all your life. You might spend a lot of money each time, but it is ecological."

He and his staff annually make about one thousand pairs in each of the two lower-priced lines as well as 175 handmade pairs in all the traditional male styles: brogues, penny and tassel loafers, Oxfords, buckles and lace-ups, boots, even golf shoes. Material includes black or brown leather, suede, cordovan, official NFL football leather, and something that looks like dimpled aluminum. At one time he made custom shoes for women, but stopped because he could not fill a typical demand: shoes in a particular style and color – for a party a few days away. For men, styles don't change much, so a few months' waiting time doesn't matter.

Daniel Day-Lewis, who played Helena Bonham Carter's fiancé in everyone's favorite film about Florence, *Room with a View*, became so intrigued with Stefano's craft that he spent almost a year working in his shop. The actor made a pair of shoes for the maestro while Stefano made shoes for Day-Lewis. Usually Stefano makes his own shoes, size 40-1/2. "I have bad feet, the same as Japanese feet, wide and short. My last is not beautiful." He also makes shoes for his wife and two sons, until the eldest, who is now ten, started school and asked for shoes like the other boys wore, the kind with flickering lights in the heels. For those, Stefano shopped at a retailer. The same lad is now coming to his father's shop on Saturday mornings, cutting simple patterns, and making leather belts.

For Stefano, ambition and curiosity have combined to create a life. "I started with a heel that was worn down; maybe it was my destiny. When I started to repair shoes, I didn't think I would make shoes. I looked at it as a job. But when I started making shoes, I discovered something very important – you are never finished learning. For made-to-measure, every pair of shoes is different; every customer has a different idea, a different fit, different problems. During every evolution, I am happy, I am excited, I want more. My work is never boring. It is a joy."

❖

Sandy's school year is drawing to a close. Creativity is complete; all that remains is the final exam, the student exhibit, and the crits. During the school year, crits are a regular part of the program, a specified time each week when students comment on each other's work in the hopes of sharing constructive advice. But the final crits, conducted by a panel of three teachers, are far more important because what they say affects the student's final mark.

Although Sandy went regularly to the school's studios on Via Nazionale, she also worked at the apartment every day, often well into the evening, and on many weekends. Because of the fragility of many of her pieces, Sandy asked for and received approval to have her crits conducted at Via Roma 3, rather than risk damage carrying everything to the studio.

Via Roma 3 has a history as a home for artists and a venue for art exhibits. In June 1974, when the building was known as Palazzo Ceci Rossi, there was a one-week show entitled *Mostra sui tetti di Firenze* (Exhibit on the Roofs of Florence). Art was displayed on our roof terrace as well on decks on two sides of the building where the rows of tiny rooms were then used as artist's garrets. Today, the units are mostly empty, but in 1974 their occupants participated in the show. The archbishop, says Erminia Luschi who attended, was not pleased because noise from the outdoor exhibit carried across the street to his residence.

Sandy's crits on March 31 are unlikely to upset the Church. Held inside, this showing is for a much smaller audience of three: OCAD coordinator and sculptor David Pellettier, resident art historian Peter Porçal, and Paulette Phillips, the OCAD faculty member who will head the 2005 fall program in Florence and has flown in for the week.

Here is what they saw of Sandy's work: eight 20 x 20 cm canvases with acrylic designs based on floor tiles; two dresses in delicately painted nylon, hemmed and wired at the edges so they hang as if their occupants have mysteriously disappeared by dancing away; two sculpted female torsos in papier mâché with wire screen mini-skirts and glass bead ornamentation; four painted panels adorned with colored flowers that look like Murano glass but were made using the bottoms of discarded water bottles; *Bella* and *Trash*, the two wire-dress sculptures created before Christmas (*Molly*, the third, hangs above her namesake's crib in Toronto); half a dozen drawings using various combinations of pencil, charcoal, and drizzled paint on pieces of brown Kraft paper measuring one meter square; three abstract drawings of the dresses done in color on glistening Mylar sheets; a dozen scenes drawn on cardboard hung on wire in plastic bags with high-fashion logos; two figures, a male and a female, sculpted from Plasticine; a scurry of nuns done in wire mesh and then covered in plaster of Paris; a Gay Nineties damsel with bustle and hat, also in plaster of Paris; two field books of sketches as well as numerous individual landscapes and city scenes in watercolor.

I cannot imagine that any of the other students at OCAD has

created as much art of such consistently high quality over this wide a range of media. Then again, Sandy has more motivation and enthusiasm to explore her inner talents than most twenty-one-year-olds who think they have so much time to spare that some of it can be wasted. The crits go well; the panel likes her work, saying it has good dramatic tension and expressing other fine phrases of the sort such people use.

Departures, as the student exhibit is called, is held at the Via Nazionale studios on a Friday night and Saturday afternoon. Sandy is represented by her two nylon hangings and three water-bottle floral designs. Interestingly enough, other than the occasional abstract painting, Sandy is one of the few students whose work could be called contemporary. The rest is mostly realistic and more traditional.

To my mind, best in show is an installation by Sarah Cullen. Entitled *The City as Written by the City,* the work fills an entire room meant to look like the office of Bronwen Cartog Perigrinus, a scientist and artist of Sarah's invention. There's a desk, ancient typewriter, a scatter of wooden furniture, and a series of large photos and small maps on the walls. Perigrinus is an alter ego for Sarah, whose middle name is Bronwen, and the room is a vehicle to let Florence explain itself through photos, found objects, and automatiste creations.

Sarah's two-part project began during the first term when she carried a small wooden box, about 20 x 30 cm, with a handle and a hinged door. Inside was suspended a pencil on a spring with weights near the tip that lightly touched paper laid on the bottom. Sarah toted the pendulum-drawing device whenever she walked or biked, causing the pen to jiggle, dance, and swing about, making erratic dots, delicate lines, and arcs. A morning's visit to the Duomo, the Uffizi, and Ponte Vecchio, for example, resulted in tracery she called maps.

The second part of the project saw her turn her small apartment into a camera obscura. The one-room apartment was actually a turret with windows on all four sides, giving a 360-degree view of the city. Sarah covered each window with a piece of black vinyl with a hole that acted as an aperture allowing light to pass through, thereby projecting the outside scene onto a piece of white canvas on an easel. "I held an inverted panoramic view of the city in my hands, one scene blending into the next," said Sarah. "Florence was on my walls, ceiling, and cupboard door." She exposed the scenes to light-sensitive paper, creating negatives from which she made positive prints, and hung them on the walls of the installation along with her maps.

While some of the students took more creative advantage of their time in Florence than others, all were affected by the experience. A few even visited ancestral homelands such as Poland, Greece, and Croatia. Everyone was infused by the sensory impact of Florence and Tuscany. "If I'd spent my fourth year in Toronto, all I would have done is go to school and commute back and forth to Thornhill," says Lenny Friedman, who graduated in the spring. "This has been a million times better."

Since our apartment is already pulsating with Sandy's art, we decide to hold a party for some of the people we've met to thank them for their friendship and to show off Sandy's creations. We send out invitations for a Sunday afternoon reception, calling it *col.tempo*, the phrase that's written on a scroll held by an old woman in a portrait by Giorgione that hangs in the Venice Accademia. The words mean "time is fleeting" so the woman is saying: Don't disparage my faded beauty because I too, once was young and you will one day be old like me.

First to arrive at 5 p.m. is Attilio Franco, Fiat 500 owner, and man about town. He has been to our apartment before and we have been out to dinner with him. Every time we see him on such social occasions he is squiring a different young woman. Sometimes he has as many as three ladies in tow. He is sixty-five; no *col.tempo* for him. Tonight's companion is Rosemary from Croatia. He brings the gift of a guest book with a hand-painted scene on a parchment cover.

Paolo Bruscoli, who participated in creating the book, arrives with his wife, Sylvia, to whom he has been married for forty years. He is puzzled by Attilio's parade of women. "He never gets past the first page. I prefer to read the whole book." Other guests include Sandy's classmates Bill, Raf, and Sarah, as well as Eileen Ebin, a Canadian who lived in Florida for the last twenty years and plans to spend a year or more in Florence learning Italian and studying art and cooking. Among the other Florentines is our patient and responsive landlord, Signor Bianchi, his wife, Roberta, and their daughter Francesca; Erminia Luschi, our Ferragamo friend; Antonio Belvedere, our favorite waiter from Paoli on Via dei Tavolini, and Kerima Arnautovic, director of Luisa Via Roma, with her ten-year-old daughter, Immran. Immran is the first to accurately identify what it was that Sandy recycled into painted flowers on canvas. Numerous adults, all asked the same question in recent days, stared until beads of sweat formed on their brows and still they could not figure out what a child knew immediately: they are the bottoms of plastic water bottles. How much insight do we lose along the way in the course of growing up?

Everybody loves Sandy's work. "What you have created is like a fantasy," is a typical comment. Across the generations, through language barriers and cultural differences, Sandy has communicated the precise message she sought to send with her art. OCAD's "official" crits and final marks are important, to be sure, but for an artist there's no higher accolade than knowing that people of any age from any heritage admire her work and understand her meaning.

Sandy gives a fine speech of welcome and thanks, saying that although she is going home soon, she will be taking a piece of everyone in her heart. Prosecco, the Villa Sandi brand designated by us as the house wine, flows. Food includes various crostini with pâté and formaggio; thinly sliced salami garnished with radish; pecorino, brie, and gorgonzola cheeses; black olives, salty cashews, and a tray of fruit pastries. Signor Bianchi is particularly taken by the pâté, calls it "tipica Toscana," and asks for the recipe. "You start with two strong legs," Sandy begins, causing him to look puzzled. His wife and daughter understand immediately that Sandy walked to the market to buy the spread; it takes the second sentence before Signor Bianchi laughs along, too. When all has been demolished, the last item served is a plate of fresh strawberries dipped in chocolate, a confection the Florentines had never before tasted. We have successfully exported something to this land where food is so celebrated.

About seven o'clock, the apartment buzzer sounds. I assume it's a late arrival so I press the button to release the front door down at the street, and wait to see who gets off the elevator. Imagine my surprise when two helmeted firemen emerge, their black slickers emblazoned with the words in large yellow print, *Vigili del Fuoco*. They are soon joined by several more firemen and a small battalion of uniformed police. Unknown to us noisy revelers, a gust of wind has ripped a window off its hinges in the neighboring vacant apartment, hurling it down onto the pavement of Via Roma where the glass shattered. No one was injured, but help has arrived to cordon off the street with metal barricades, secure the remaining windows, and ensure there are no further calamities.

The sudden clamor of uniformed men in our midst reminds me of the scene in "A Child's Christmas in Wales" by Dylan Thomas after the fire brigade has successfully doused a blaze in the living room of the Prothero residence. Three tall firemen in their shining helmets are standing amid the debris when Miss Prothero, who is described as always knowing the right thing to say, peers into the smoke-filled room and asks: "Would you like anything to read?" In the current circumstances, I have a different question, one that is more likely to appeal to this crew: "Would you like anything to eat?"

❖❖❖

Of all the holidays celebrated in Italy, the most unusual must be April 25. When I first heard that all banks and many shops would close on Monday to celebrate the liberation of Italy I assumed the tribute must be about Garibaldi and the fight for independence that led to unification in 1861. But, no, this turns out to be the sixtieth anniversary of the liberation of Italy from the Nazis. A question forms on my lips: But weren't you on the same side? Wisely, I keep quiet, following the advice of Harrison McCain, the New Brunswick businessman who dominated the world's French fry market. He once said that the secret to his global success was, "Drink the local wine and make no comparisons."

In a country that's wall-to-wall monuments, there is nothing anywhere to commemorate the Second World War. The only references to that era are the plaques that appear, in some cities, listing the Italian partisans who died fighting Mussolini's Fascists and Hitler's Nazis from 1943 to 1945. Today's parade is the shortest I have seen so far. Any other march had mustered up to two hundred men and women garbed in medieval costumes; this one manages only four. The mayor leads the procession that comprises one brass and woodwind band and less than one hundred civilians, including ten veterans in street clothes wearing plumed or Alpine hats. There is no representation of the Allied troops who battled their way across Sicily and up the boot, no mention of the nineteen thousand Americans and six thousand Canadians killed during that terrible twenty-month campaign. It's as if Italy somehow liberated itself.

About one-third of the participants in today's march support a banner saying: Save the Constitution. Without them, the parade would have taken a mere five minutes to pass any given point. With them, it took seven. Parades in Milan and Rome are reportedly larger – Rome, because it is the capital and Milan because that's where they hanged Mussolini.

Other contingents are made up of members from the Fascist and Communist parties, more conundrums in a country already filled with riddles. Prime Minister Silvio Berlusconi is forever haranguing the Communists as if the Cold War is not over, yet his coalition government includes Mussolini's political heirs in the Alleanza Nazionale party. Mussolini's granddaughter, Alessandra, is an Italian deputy and leads her own right-wing party.

More meaningful is the Victory in Europe ceremony a few days later in Repubblica. The piazza looks like a proper parade square with veterans and uniformed troops formed up on all four sides, facing inward. The most impressive group are the nurses who wear gloves, flowing purple head coverings, and starched white uniforms with a red cross and medals on the chest. A military band plays while the red, white, and green Italian flag is raised, and officers salute. V-E Day is specific and understood, very different from the selective memories of the liberation parade, where the baggage of history weighs heavy.

❖❖

A visit to Leonardo da Vinci's *The Last Supper* in Milan begins with a forty-five-minute session on the Internet. Only one thousand viewers a day are admitted, in groups of twenty-five, each group given a mere fifteen minutes to view Leonardo's most famous fresco. Such observational brevity is becoming prevalent. In Florence, the Brancacci Chapel has a fifteen-minute limit to see Masaccio's Adam and Eve being expelled from the Garden of Eden. The record, however, must go to the Palazzo Medici-Riccardi where ten people at a time are allowed only seven minutes with Benozzo Gozzoli's frescoes showing *The Journey of the Magi* riding on horses down the hill from Fiesole.

The official Leonardo *Last Supper* website shows no ticket availability in April and only a few singles spotted throughout May. There's plenty of choice in July, but we want to go next week. So much for paying the cheap and cheerful admission price of 6.50 euros, and welcome to the world of the ticket broker, the business that used to be known by its more accurate moniker, scalping. Just as you can procure tickets for any sold-out concert or sports event, as long as you're prepared to pay the inflated fee, so too is Leonardo readily available. One method is to sign up for a day-long city tour, with a guaranteed stop included, but we want to set our own pace and see our own sights.

I poke around among the various possibilities, finally settling on a website called Florence Art, because they will e-mail a voucher that I can print out and use to collect our tickets at the site a few minutes before the designated time. There seems to be a choice of date and time, so I request 3 p.m. next Wednesday, give credit card details for the 31.40 euro total – about C$50 for the two tickets or two-and-a-half times the box office price – and hit the send key. Sure enough, I get a quick e-mail reply

saying my order has been received but will not be complete until the voucher comes within thirty-six hours. The voucher duly arrives, but it is not for the 3 p.m. slot that appeared to be available. That's sold out; we have been assigned 6 p.m. I'm glad I waited to buy our train tickets. We'll be returning on the 8 p.m. train, and won't get home until midnight, but that's okay. Next to opera at La Scala, we've got Milan's toughest ticket.

In fact, it's amazing there's anything left at all to see on the wall of the refectory at Santa Maria delle Grazie. Leonardo, otherwise a technical wizard, decided for this commission completed in 1498 that he would use an entirely new method. Frescos are usually painted on wet plaster so an artist only works on a small area at a time, the *giornata* (daily portion), which dries overnight thus permanently embedding the colors. Leonardo painted instead onto dry plaster with disastrous results. In less than twenty years, his work was peeling off the wall. Over the next two hundred years Leonardo's *Last Supper* was repainted three times. Conservation work carried out after the Second World War and a further twenty-year restoration that ended in 1999 does make you wonder how much of the original actually remains.

Yet here we are, eagerly gathering a few minutes before the designated 6 p.m., with a group that includes an airport-bound woman hauling three pieces of luggage. We slide our coded tickets into an electronic reading device and then move into the first of three holding tanks. In each area, the doors through which we pass must close before the next set opens, as if we are entering a disease-control center. At least the view is grand. The enclosures have glass on three sides so we can admire the convent cloister and the unusual dome of Santa Maria delle Grazie, with its stacked and floating circles designed by the architect Bramante.

The final set of doors opens into the sanctum sanctorum, an empty former refectory about as wide as a tennis court and twice as long. On the right, stretching across the end wall, measuring 460 x 880 cm (15 x 29 feet) and looking far more vibrant and lively than it deserves to, is Leonardo's *The Last Supper*, the form and figures engraved into my brain from seeing so many reproductions over the years.

Beyond the fresco's innate beauty and the miracle of its survival, what matters about this version of *The Last Supper* is that Leonardo altered the tradition. Previously, Judas had always been placed on the long side of the table closest to the viewer, sitting alone. Typical is the version in San Marco in Florence by Ghirlandaio who added on the floor beside the isolated Judas a black cat, a symbol of evil that further foreshadows the betrayal to come. Another fine example of the earlier genre is Andrea del Castagno's masterpiece in the convent of Sant'Apollonia in Florence where no advance ticket is required and admission is free so hardly anyone bothers to visit.

In all of those earlier renditions, nothing is happening. What Leonardo did for the first time was to show the very moment when Christ announces that one among them will betray him. As a result, Leonardo shows the apostles reacting with varying degrees of anger and disbelief. Christ is about to identify the betrayer by handing him a piece of bread dipped in wine so

Leonardo had to move Judas from "our" side of the table to sit on His right where he'd be handy. Judas is the only disciple who does not look surprised. He is partially in shadow, his left hand open, ready to receive; Christ's right hand is empty, but he is reaching for the sop.

There is also a more modern interpretation of Leonardo's work. Anyone who has read Dan Brown's *The Da Vinci Code* will look at the other disciple to Christ's right and say, hmm, maybe Brown is right. Maybe that's not a sweet, effeminate John. It could be Mary Magdalene; perhaps she and Christ did marry and have a child. Thus distracted, you begin to notice other oddities: the arched doorway monks cut through the wall that chopped off Christ's feet; the apparent miscue in the perspective where three small squares hanging on the right-hand wall seem off line; the sharp creases in the tablecloth that show how small it was folded while stored.

On a side wall hangs a series of lights like those that signal the start of a drag race. When they're all lit, our time's up. With one light still to go, and maybe a minute remaining, an attendant herds us toward the exit at the far end of the room even as the next group spills into the space. The other fresco, a crucifixion by Giovanni Donato Montorfano, barely attracts a glance as we pass through the final series of holding pens and sliding doors that lead outside. Damn you anyway, Dan Brown; you've hijacked one of Leonardo's best-known works.

MAY

M AY DAY IS WORKERS' DAY, when marchers take to the
streets in Berlin and Moscow, Havana and Hong Kong,
demanding better wages and working conditions. In Saint
Peter's Square, many of the fifty thousand pilgrims wear
yellow scarves to mark their solidarity with CISL, the Catholic
trade union. "I hope that the young, especially, will not want for
work, and that working conditions will be ever more respectful
of the dignity of the human person," says Benedict XVI in his
first Angelus blessing.

Prayers are about all that remains. Just this week Prime
Minister Berlusconi revised downward Italy's 2005 growth
forecasts to an anemic 1.2 per cent as Italy slips into recession.
An estimated 3 million young people call themselves "the pre-
carious" because they have temporary jobs with low pay, high
turnover, and no holidays or benefits. They could not take the
time off work to march, so we didn't see them.

In the past week the weather has gone from high spring to

high summer, sunny, hot, and 27°C. We spy a poster announcing *Toscana Esclusiva*, which appears to offer access to a garden but gives no location, only a telephone number. I call, the man asks where I am, I say Piazza del Duomo, and he tells me to come to Piazza Antinori, just three blocks away, for more information. The site turns out to be one of seventeen palazzos and gardens open to the public today with a city map provided for a self-guided walking tour.

Throughout our time in Florence we've often paused at passageways to peer through locked wrought-iron gates, trying to imagine what the interior courtyard might look like. For the past two weeks we've admired wisteria vines cascading over the tops of walls and wondered about the other flowering delights in the concealed garden. Today's our chance to find out. If you were holidaying in Florence for only three days you might not bother with this tenth annual open house, but we spend a glorious six hours on a Sunday walking, from the magnificent courtyard of Palazzo Ximènes Panciatichi in the east end, to Palazzo Pandolfini with its Greek statuary and orangerie in the north, to Palazzo Frescobaldi near Santo Spirito with its sloping garden giving views of the Arno.

There are atriums with skylights and stained glass, family crests and busts, fountains and frescos. Graceful stairways lead to ballrooms with Murano glass chandeliers. These gardens are not the formal Italianate style found at villas with rigorous layouts, trimmed boxwood, and long water. They are smaller and high-walled so they're more casual, with pebbled walkways, a few specimen magnolia, pine, or palm trees, some flowering spring shrubs such as azalea, rhododendron, and camellia, early roses and irises, purple wisteria as well as an unusual white variety, orange and lemon trees bearing fruit, grottos, and statuary. They are the kinds of places where you'd like to be hired on as a helper, and if they didn't want to pay you, well, that would be fine, too. We see fifteen of the seventeen sites on the list, with a brief stop for lunch, before collapsing at 4 p.m., our heads filled with the private splendor that's usually hidden from public view.

✧✦✧

The first thing you notice about Angela Caputi is that she is wearing neither earrings nor a necklace. I don't normally pay much attention to a woman's jewelry, unless the stone in her ring is so huge you can't help but stare, but in this case there is a reason: Angela Caputi has created a line of high-fashion costume jewelry that's sold round the world.

The reason she wears nothing near her face may be because everything is concentrated on her hands through which so much creativity flows. She has a vintage ring on every finger, bangles on both wrists, and three watches, two set on local time, and one for New York.

Her high-fashion jewelry, sold under the Angela Caputi Giuggiù label, is contemporary in design, eclectic in style, and uses synthetic materials and plastics. Initially, she looked to cinema and the theater for inspiration, but now ideas come from everywhere. "Style changes every night. I am always searching for something new as well as pleasure from color and material," she says. A necklace available in three different lengths may combine black beads, molded red geometric pieces, and tassels. Another model is made with clear aurora borealis beads and chunky donut discs, all pieces light for easy wearing. For the wrist there are bangles and cuffs or bracelets with faux semi-precious stones. As for pins, how about a flower with four petals made of Lucite in topaz or lilac? Everything is proudly labeled Made in Italy and each piece is hand-assembled by six women working on tables covered in green felt right in her shop on Via Santo Spirito.

Half of Angela's annual sales are in exports, mostly to the United States and Japan, although she also sells through outlets in Ottawa and Montreal. Retail prices of her goods in Italy are twice the wholesale price, so they are mostly in the range of 100 to 200 euros, but they rise sharply in other countries. In New York the three stores on Madison Avenue that carry her goods sell at triple the wholesale price; in Japan the wholesale price is quadrupled. Still, compared to some costume jewelry, prices are reasonable, so her clientele – most of whom are twenty-five or older – are not wealthy.

Angela has eleven employees working in three shops, two in Florence and one in Milan, but her favorite is on Via Santo Spirito where display space is open, dozens of shallow drawers reveal hundreds of different styles, and her glass-walled office lets her keep an eye on the showroom floor. Since launching the business thirty years ago she has always had her workshop and office here in the Oltrarno – which means "the other side of the Arno" – south of the river. This is Florence's historic "new" town that had its beginnings in the twelfth century when the original city grew larger. Market gardens and olive groves were taken over by artisans who relied on the patronage of merchants, mill owners, and woolen manufacturers who needed goods on which to spend their money: furniture, tapestries, frescos, bronze door hardware, silver tableware, chandeliers, and picture frames. Even today, as you walk the narrow streets around Santo Spirito and San Frediano, artisan shops abound, everything from hole-in-the-wall ateliers to elegant space occupied by retailers like Angela.

Stylish in a flowing black dress, with a warm, motherly manner and gray hair pulled back in a bun, Angela is sixty-seven and shows no signs of retiring. Why should she? She has created her own international business and intends to carry on for some time yet. Drop in on a Saturday afternoon and she will likely be there, working on the sales floor with the other clerks. "I will never leave it," she says. "It takes a great deal of courage to be free in one's work, but it is the most important thing in life."

Col.tempo, our Sunday afternoon art show and reception in April, has launched an amazing chain of events. Kerima, director of Luisa Via Roma, raved to her colleagues about Sandy's work. She brings Doris, the Viennese wife of the owner, Andrea Panconesi, to see the creations. Doris announces that she wants to display two of Sandy's wire-dress sculptures in the store window. Sandy cannot believe her good fortune. After they leave, she says, "It's a dream come true."

Luisa Via Roma began thirty-five years ago as a hat shop run by Luisa, the grandmother of Andrea, who represents the third generation of the family. Since Andrea took over twenty years ago, he has created a vast enterprise with two floors of retail space offering men's and women's fashion from top labels such as Yamamoto, Missoni, Antonio Marras, and Jean Paul Gaultier. Andrea bought some of the apartments in our building as they came on the market and he now owns half of them. The suites have been converted into various uses: a kitchen on the second floor to prepare food for events and receptions, space on our floor to hold excess goods in the run-up to busy seasons, offices for staff on the fifth floor, as well as workrooms for seamstresses who do alterations.

A few weeks after we arrived, Sandy met Kerima on the elevator and the two quickly became good friends. Kerima, a beautiful redhead with a lively personality, moved to Florence from Dubrovnik seventeen years ago. In addition to her mother tongue, Croatian, she also speaks Italian, French, and English. You know when Kerima's at the store because her bicycle is parked in the street outside in the typical Florentine fashion with both wheels tucked against the curb, one pedal flat and fixed on the sidewalk, so the bike stands erect on its own without needing a kickstand or any other support.

Kerima arranged for us to attend one of Luisa's evening receptions during the Pitti Immagine Uomo in January. Florence used to be the fashion center of Italy but made a mistake thirty years ago by not building an international airport, so the fashion industry slowly migrated north to Milan. This semiannual men's wear show is the only major fashion trade fair still held in Florence, a time when the city fills with designers, buyers, and models. One evening we were among the beautiful people with coveted invitations sashaying past the ogling crowd on the rope line to join the festivities inside.

Once Doris decided that Luisa Via Roma wanted Sandy's dresses, the project was turned over to Chris Scott, who each week designs the shop windows. Chris, thirty, was born in Rochester, N.Y., worked in New York City and Los Angeles, and has been in Florence for about a year. He visits the apartment twice to see the dresses, take photos, and ponder the eventual presentation.

For Sandy, having her work in this particular window is the ultimate accolade for her time in Italy. Here are some thoughts Sandy wrote during the period just before installation: "Fantasia in Florence will have reached its pinnacle when I see my dresses hung in the window of Luisa Via Roma. Who would have believed that I could do it – create a body of work that had something to say to others and have so much fun in its creation. I pushed myself to the limit to see just what I could do and learned so much about myself in the process. Looking at familiar things through a new prism, expressing materiality, doing things I'd never done before yet realizing partway along that I had to give myself permission to experiment and explore. Permission is a big issue for us all – I came to realize that it was all right to take my turn – to explore myself, discover the depths of my creativity and to do it at this time of life gives one a new lease on life, ageless and timeless.

"It's quite a feeling for a Guelph girl who did the windows at Reitmans as a teenager! Reitmans offered me a full-time job when I finished high school but I went to teacher's college instead. Funny, isn't it, that forty-five years later I'm adorning a window in Italy with my creations. I've either come a long way or no distance at all, depending on how you look at it. As an artist it is very affirming for me to have created something that communicates a feeling of fantasy to people."

The two dresses, *Bella* and *Trash*, were hung in the window on a Wednesday night along with a strapless blue chiffon evening dress by Chloé on a mannequin. On the rear wall are painted swooping circles in pink and red; on the side wall are the words:

Fantasia
le sculture di
Sandy McQueen.

Next morning, curious passersby come into Luisa Via Roma expressing interest. Kerima suggests Sandy have some business cards printed for the store to hand out. Attilio Franco comes to the rescue. Sandy visits his studio, supplies the text, and chooses the paper and a typeface. Twenty-four hours later Attilio delivers to the door one hundred business cards that are passed along to the store. Every time we go out, we admire *Bella* and *Trash*, two old friends who are now appearing in an incredible new upscale locale.

The whole process, from private reception to Sandy's first public exhibition, took less than three weeks. "This is your destiny, but sometimes your destiny needs a little push," says

Kerima, who was a guiding hand behind the scenes through-out. Replies Sandy, "You are my dreamweaver."

⊶⊷

With less than two weeks remaining until our flight home to Toronto, we no longer save everything. After eight months of keeping every piece of paper in case we might need an address again and retaining every item gleaned in the streets that could make art, the time has come to prune. Out goes that old dryer vent that might have become part of a sculpture. Gone are those wooden boxes that no longer look like treasures. Of our four Italian-English phrase books, Collins has been the most helpful; we toss away the other three. Turtlenecks badly mangled by the washing machine become casualties of the weight limit on the return flight. The two-volume set of the complete works of Italian sculptor Fausto Melotti is far more essential.

Sandy returns from an errand, speaking poetic words that she has composed in her head. "I am but here a speck of time. As grains of sand upon a seashore drift to land so, too, do others float in to fill my place." We spend the better part of three days packing clothing, art, and memorabilia. There's no trouble finding ten sturdy cardboard boxes for the task; everything we need is right outside our door on Via Roma where cardboard discarded by shops is picked up daily by city trucks before 10 a.m. Our boxes come courtesy of Miss Sixty and Massimo Dutti. We call a shipper and send everything via ocean freight not knowing if or when we will see these goods again. We do not even have our own house to go to; we will be living with our daughter, Alison, while we see what's available in the real estate market.

In the final few days, we visit some places we've been meaning to see and attend several annual events that come along. A day trip by bus to Panzano in Chianti is made possible because the SITA ticket agent cautions us that there will be a strike at 5 p.m. We amble about the village, enjoy the panoramic views, have a tasty lunch of bruschetta, ribollita soup, and grilled lamb followed by tartufo and coffee at Oltre il Giardino, and then catch an earlier bus back to Florence than we might have otherwise taken, grateful to have been forewarned.

We spend another day drifting, which is walking without a destination. We cross Ponte Vecchio, go through Piazza Santa Felicita, climb the steep Costa San Giorgio, one of the prettiest streets in Florence, go by Fort Belvedere, traipse along Via di San Leonardo and walk all around the rim of the valley with sweeping views of the city, past San Miniato al Monte, the first church we visited last September, to Piazzale Michelangelo where amid the busloads of tourists three couples are having their wedding portraits taken with the panorama of Florence as a beautiful backdrop.

In the lee of the lookout on a gently sloping hill amid an olive grove there's an iris show, an annual event begun in 1957 that showcases thousands of the stately flowers on their proud stems. Stone pathways lead past mounded beds exploding with the familiar blue, white, purple, and yellow blooms in various combinations but there's also black and chocolate and a triple iris that's as big as the late Queen Mum's hat. The prizewinners from other years have lyrical names – Honky Tonk Blues, Kilt Tilt, Babbling Brook, Spun Gold, Sable Night, Shipshape, Dream Lover, Before the Storm, Silverado, Pink Taffeta – from an alphabet of countries, Australia to the United States. Also spotted about are redbud and roses, a pond of pink water lilies, unusual orange poppies, bridal wreath, deutzia, columbine, wispy French tamarisk, and white rock cress so thick and prolific it almost forms a hedge. Creatures live here, too: skittish lizards, bumblebees, butterflies, and the biggest flying grasshopper this side of Texas. This is a garden that appeals to multiple senses: the sight of the colors, the smell of their perfume, the sound of trilling blackbirds, and the touch of warm sun and a light breeze on the skin.

Another day we attend an arts and crafts show at the Fortezza da Basso, a sixteenth-century fortress north of the train station that's now used for trade fairs. The show sprawls through half a dozen buildings behind the turrets and parapets with goods ranging from Peruvian trinkets to Perugian furniture. We run into goldsmith Paulo Penco and his wife, Beatrice, who are also there to look, and Irma Schwegler, who has taken a booth to sell her handmade clothing bearing the Old Fashion label. Florence feels like a small town. Whenever you're out, you always see someone you know.

For months I've been trying to work up the courage to eat *trippa alla fiorentina*, a local specialty. Tripe is made from cow's stomach, okay? I almost ordered tripe in a restaurant once but when I asked for more details about the preparation the waitress's lip curled so badly as she began that I backed off. Every time I went food shopping in Alimentary Alley I walked through Piazza dei Cimatori where a wagon sells tripe. I must have eyed that wagon fifty times, every time thinking how everyone had told me that the wagon in Cimatori had the best *trippa alla fiorentina* in the city. Everyone also warned me I wouldn't like it. I listened to both. I never did get around to tasting *trippa* and I can't say I wish I had.

We make a return visit to the walled garden at the Palazzo del Vivarelli Colonna, the oasis we went to on the last day of our first month in Florence, the day the garden closed for the season. Now open again, the garden is a familiar place, like spending time fondly with an old friend. There are lemons in abundance, and purple and yellow pansies, as well as azalea bushes in pink, red, and orange. Sweet peas and roses are coming along but we will not see them in bloom. The fountain swan still holds the writhing snake; the sea grotto looks as intriguing as ever. We sit on the same bench as we did in September and think back on all that has happened to us, none of which we could possibly have imagined.

✧✦✧

At a time like this, you wonder: Could we live here forever? Several months back, I learned enough about the difficulty of buying property in Italy to know that it's not a decision to be taken lightly. Of course, you could rent a place and stay for the rest of your days, but Peter Porçal's experience living in Florence for more than thirty years raises a cautionary flag. "You can never be part of the society. If you go away for a while and come back, you have to get used to it again. It is not like coming home," he told me over lunch. "There is a limit to how far you can identify yourself with a country in which you were not born." Anyway, I could never look as good as one of those Italian stallions on parade. Put me in a tight-fitting t-shirt and I'd more likely evoke levity not lusty comments. I'm more of a cardigan guy. No, we will not stay, but we will return. Again and again. Sandy has already made arrangements to come back for a month to work with several artisans as she takes her wire dresses to the next level.

No one can understand any new country in nine months, but by stepping outside our everyday lives, we did learn something about ourselves. Italy changed us in ways both small and large. When we lived in England and visited a village church, I always sought out the information sheet, often printed on a wooden paddle, so I could make certain I saw everything that someone else said mattered. I didn't want anyone to say later, "Oh, you visited St. Malcolm among the Maudlins. Did you see Sir Mortimer's tomb, the one with his thumbs in the glass jar?" For all my head-down effort, reading rather than just looking around, no one ever asked me such a question.

In Italy, looking with knowledge is welcome, but I often just let the surroundings seep through my skin and go deep into my soul. Details may be forgotten, but the warmth of such feelings can forever be summoned on a blustery winter's night. Someone once said, "The past is history, the future is mystery, and the present is a gift." After living in Florence, I now know not only what that means but why that philosophy matters.

As for the larger changes in our lives, Sandy discovered that her creativity knows no bounds, that she has her own unique artistic voice, and that she can create beauty from wire, paints, plaster of Paris, charcoal, screening, beads, bottle bottoms – anything she chooses. For my part, I learned that I can easily live without the public profile of my picture on a newspaper column or my byline on some magazine article that the world will little note nor long remember.

We learned the importance of keeping family close, honoring the work of others, and constantly being curious about the world around. We learned not to envy anyone, to cultivate friendships, and to spend time each day on tasks that have intrinsic value. We learned to treasure the Italian way of life that marvels in the moment, celebrates youth and age alike, and treats strangers generously and with respect. We learned that taking risks in life can offer great rewards. But most of all, we learned that while we do not require as much as we previously believed by way of living space or material possessions, we do need each other. On our fortieth wedding anniversary in March, we two high school sweethearts bought a small brass padlock, wrote our initials and the date on it with a black marker, and secured the lock with the dozens of other similar sentimental statements on the wrought-iron railing beneath the statue of goldsmith Benvenuto Cellini on Ponte Vecchio, the oldest bridge across the Arno, the one lined with modern-day jewelers and goldsmith shops. The tradition is relatively recent. Couples have been declaring their love for each other in this manner and at this location for about ten years. Once the lock was in place, we threw the keys into the Arno. Until death us do part.

◈◈

The secret to understanding Italy may be this: the country might not work but everything functions. Strikes make appropriate statements, but travelers can still move about. The daily parade allows a participation in society, a time of choosing sides, declaring what you believe in or are against while others can pay attention or not, as they wish. Governments are corrupt, but everybody knows, so how much does it matter? Streets and intersections are a chaotic vortex of scooters, cars, and bicycles, but drivers are civil, vehicles move along, there is little road rage. And fantasies can come true, as Sandy has proven. "Italy is like the cartoons; everything is possible," says Kerima. "And you are never bored."

Italians are rightly proud of their country and are forever asking: Have you visited Lucca or Volterra or Cortona? They recommend their favorite restaurants, call to say that an interesting exhibit just opened or a concert is coming on the weekend. There was so much to see and think about that in the nine months we were here I filled four of those ninety-six-page lined Moleskin notebooks with my cramped script. At home, I'm lucky to fill one such notebook in a year. There might have been one grumpy salesclerk somewhere, but for the most part, everyone we met was cheerful, helpful, generous, and in love with life.

The food was wonderful, everything always so fresh. When

we lived in England, we enjoyed the citrus from Spain, but Italy refuses to import Spanish fruit because it's sprayed, preferring instead untreated fruit from Sardinia and Sicily. We almost became vegetarians and made our own hearty winter soups starting with onion, garlic, and chicken stock, and then adding water, chopped celery, carrots, potatoes, zucchini, white beans, tiny buttons of pasta, porcini mushrooms, and whatever else looked good that day. When Erminia Luschi was felled by the flu, Sandy ferried in bowls of homemade soup for two days, and Erminia swears she quickly got better as a result.

Our best restaurant meal by far was at Villa San Michele in Fiesole. The building began as a fifteenth-century monastery, boasts a façade by Michelangelo, was owned for a time by American financier Henry White Cannon, and has been a hotel since 1982. The views of Florence are stunning, the food first class. A close second is Beccofino, which is more modern than most Florentine restaurants, and has the distinct advantage over Villa San Michele of being within easy walking distance back along Santa Trinità Bridge where the moon always seems to shine on the Arno. Villa San Michele's van takes you there but it's a thirty-euro cab ride home. Everyone recommends Mario, near the central market, so the lunchtime lineups are long but the food is ordinary and the interior is dark and cramped. Osteria Belle Donne, where tables are also communal, is much better. One time, a woman sitting beside us asked, "Isn't this Heaven?" I was already in Paradise, even before sitting down.

❖

Italy is the garden of Europe, Tuscany the garden of Italy, and Florence the flower of Tuscany, goes a childhood Florentine saying. Of all the vistas the most beautiful for me was the one I saw daily out our apartment window as I sat writing at the library table. I am there, right now, gazing in wonderment at its beauty even after all these many months.

Across the street on the sidewalk below is a newsstand run by the hardest-working couple in Italy. They arrive before 6:30 a.m., unlock the stall door and raise the shutters, then spend the next hour scrubbing the sidewalk, washing the exterior, and setting out newspapers, postcards, guidebooks, and confectionary items in wire display racks. More than thirteen hours later, at 7:45 p.m., the day is over but only after the set-up has been reversed, the goods have all been safely stowed inside for the night, and the shutters closed. Six days a week they toil; on Sundays they rest. Their son was supposed to help out and eventually take over the business, but he constantly slept in and showed up late, so they told him not to bother anymore.

The newsstand is tucked against the wall of the Archbishop's Palace, a graceful stone and stucco building of relatively recent vintage, erected in 1896. Ground floor tenants on our side are two clothing retailers, Patrizia Pepe and Ruffo. In both shops, staff members daily polish the glass and vacuum the floors of the windows; displays are discreetly changed every week behind drapery until ready to be revealed. In a third-floor apartment lives an elderly woman who keeps an ever-changing array of potted flowers on her two window ledges. She and her cat will often sit together, looking out the open window, watching the world go by. On Sundays her son comes for lunch. She cooks and prepares for his visit all morning. He wears his good suit and they eat at a round wooden table that's visible through the slightly parted white lace curtains. You can almost read their lips as the conversation continues long into the afternoon.

On the roof of the Archbishop's Palace, directly at my eye level, hang three bells in an architectural element with a broken pediment and a thin metal cross. A pair of jackdaws, elegant in their gray-and-black morning coats, often perch on the pediment and preen each other lovingly. Beyond the tiled roofs and treed terraces rises the octagonal dome of the Medici Chapels whose siren call did bid us come. Construction was still not finished 140 years after work began, when the family of wealthy patrons finally petered out in 1743. To the right of the chapels are the arched loggia, melodic bells, and delicate spire of the church of San Lorenzo. With every ringing of those bells, or the bells of Giotto's Campanile, Sandy and I always stop whatever we're doing to listen in quiet contemplation. As for the lantern on top of the Duomo, scaffolding hides it still.

The sky is blue and the sun is shining. I'm looking out the window, trying to say goodbye, but I cannot. So I quietly whisper *ciao*. No formal *arrivederla* for this view. After all, Florence has become our friend. A few of her secret places were revealed to us; some of her special people opened their hearts. This view will be with us forever. And the sky will always be blue.

Acknowledgements

Everyone we met in Florence was warm, welcoming, and willing to tell us what they knew or show us what they did. A few Florentines, however, deserve special mention. The gentle and generous Paolo Bruscoli not only spent hours with us in his workshop but he also introduced us to his many friends among the local artisans. Roberto Bianchi, our elegant landlord, went out of his way to make us feel at home. Once, when we mistakenly locked ourselves out, he jumped on his scooter in Impruneta and twenty minutes later was at Via Roma 3 to let us in. Erminia Luschi, who invited us to her apartment countless times, was a wonderful cook and invaluable guide to the best shops for everything from pasta to *olio nuovo*. Peter Porçal, OCAD's dynamic local art historian, taught us everything we learned about the Renaissance. The vivacious Kerima Arnautovic, director of Luisa Via Roma, was a dream maker. The surprise visit by our son Mark, daughter-in-law Andrea, and granddaughter Molly was a loving reminder of the importance of family in our lives.

In Toronto, our thanks go to the indefatigable Linda McKnight who found a home for the manuscript, as well as publisher Kim McArthur about whom I can't say enough. There was also exemplary work from a pair of professionals: designer Linda Pellowe and copy editor Pamela Erlichman. Our art historian daughter, Dr. Alison McQueen, read the manuscript, made numerous insightful comments, and did some helpful translations; another reader, Eric Reguly, Rome-based correspondent for the *Globe and Mail*, found a few bloopers about the country of his birth.

But of all the people involved, Sandy deserves the greatest praise. Both Florence and the book were her idea; without her illustrations there would be little luster to my words.

Rod McQueen
March 2007